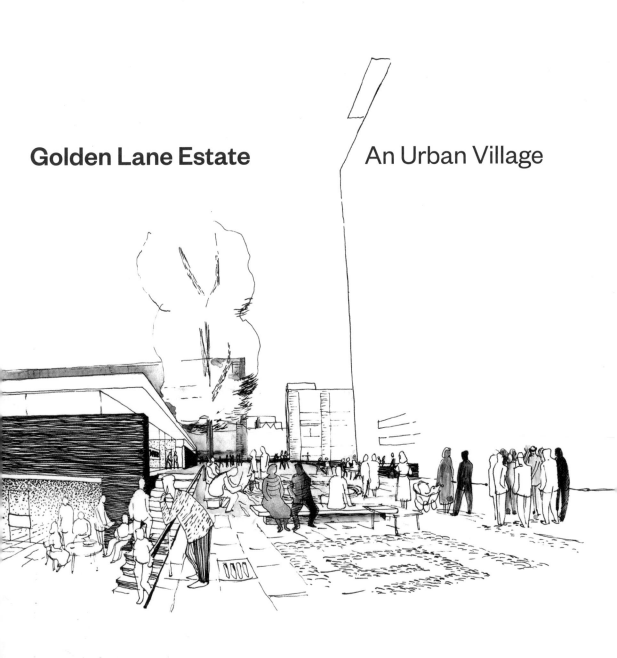

Golden Lane Estate

An Urban Village

Golden Lane Estate

An Urban Village

BATSFORD

Photography
Mary Gaudin
Julian Ward

Contents

Foreword

Stefi Orazi

A month before my 30th birthday, I moved into the Golden Lane Estate with my then partner. It was our first home together. After the initial realization of how much renovation the flat needed, we soon became obsessed with its idiosyncratic details: a three-quarter-height partition wall with uplighters integrated into the top; built-in wardrobes with more drawers than anyone with a sock fetish could dream of; a little two-way cupboard next to the front door for milk deliveries; unique cast aluminium door numbers; huge full-width timber windows that pivoted in the centre for easy cleaning—the list goes on. Every detail had been thoroughly considered, and as a whole, made the flat utterly charming.

We soon got ourselves involved in the residents' association. It was at a time when there was an influx of young creatives moving onto the estate, and the long-standing residents' association embraced this new younger generation and, in fact, wanted to attract more of us to join. I volunteered to become the association's graphic designer and produced leaflets and posters to encourage new members. Through this process, I met lots of the residents and many have become life-long friends.

I lived on the estate for nearly ten years, and in three different types of flats, each unique in character, and in each the hand of Chamberlin, Powell and Bon could be felt. It is this relationship with the architecture and its architects that makes the estate feel so personal, and my attachment to it, as with many residents, is an emotional one. It was, therefore, with a degree of reservation that when I was approached by Batsford to create this book, I agreed to take it on. During the time I lived there, I saw a decline in the maintenance of the buildings. The once regular cyclical works programme seemed to

have been abandoned, the promise of new windows across the estate was regularly shelved and delayed. Residents had begun to become increasingly frustrated and their voices not listened to. I knew that interviewing residents for this book would not be an easy listen (it's worth mentioning that my request to interview the estate management for this project was declined). Of course, this is not a problem unique to Golden Lane: any estate, particularly one that is coming up to 70 years old and is Grade II and Grade II* listed, faces the challenge of how to bring it up to 21st-century standards, especially within the constraints of a limited budget. In many ways, it has fared better than other council estates due to the quality of its design and wealthy central London location, and it has not faced the antisocial behaviour some estates have.

Many of the original residents have sadly passed away since I first moved there, and this is a very different book to one that would have been made a decade ago. The sense of community, however, is still very strong—and like nowhere else I have experienced before or since. With the successful refurbishment of the community centre a few years ago, and the recladding of the Great Arthur House tower recently, the estate has been given a new lease of life. With firm plans for an estate-wide upgrade of the windows now in place, I hope that Golden Lane is now given the attention it deserves, and that the City of London seeks the knowledge of the people who know and care for it most—its residents.

Introduction   Elain Harwood

The History of the Golden Lane Estate

Golden Lane, running north from the City of London's boundary, was first developed in the thirteenth century. The dominant feature by the late sixteenth century was a brewery, which stood amid small houses and shops roughly on the site of Stanley Cohen House and the lawn behind it (fig. 2). A second, far larger, brewery was later added on the corner of Old Street; with the Brewers Hall and Whitbread's brewery also close by, the area must have been awash with beer.[1] Otherwise, Richard Horwood's map of 1792–9 (fig. 3) suggests that Golden Lane had similarities with present-day Whitecross Street, which runs parallel to the east. To the west, behind the brewery, there lay a jumble of short residential terraces between the slightly grander Bridgewater Square to the south and the more orderly Hatfield Street to the north. To meet the demand of the expanding city, lots of local builders had developed tiny plots of land, leaving open space between them and creating a singularly haphazard, incoherent maze of culs-de-sac and alleyways.

The open spaces did not last long. As the breweries fell into the hands of a few large companies from the mid-nineteenth century onwards and their number was rationalized, so the area became the centre of London's rag trade, with showrooms, warehouses and factories. *The Builder* magazine in March 1879 reported that Golden Lane was about to be doubled in width on its west side and rebuilt with 'large warehouses and business premises', following a similar operation nearing completion along Fann Street.[2] These warehouses were noted for their deep basements — and for the combustible nature of their goods. A fire on the night of 19 November 1897 swept away 4 acres (1.6 hectares) of similar properties on Jewin Street and Jewin Crescent, further south in the heart of present-day Barbican, and the entire area burned merrily in the air raids of 1940–1.[3] The most damaging of these raids occurred on 29 December 1940, when for three hours high-explosive bombs, incendiaries and parachute mines rained across the streets north of St Paul's Cathedral. Overall, the war destroyed a third of the City, a third of its buildings and a quarter of its rateable value; but damage was concentrated in its northern and eastern wards, with almost every building in Barbican and Moorgate areas destroyed.[4] In the square of land between Fann and Hatfield streets, Goswell Road and Golden Lane, only one building survived, the premises of Maurice Rosenberg, skirt manufacturer, at No.40 Fann Street on the corner of Hotwater Court.[5] The rest of the site became a dumping ground for rubble cleared from the surrounding streets.

The Golden Lane Competition

The City of London boundary cut across Golden Lane, and so the site off Fann Street was subject to the strictures of both the London County Council (LCC), as overall planning authority, and the City of London Corporation. The *County of London Plan* produced by J H Forshaw and Patrick Abercrombie for the LCC in 1943 proposed a continued business use for the area, as in 1944 did the Corporation's *City of London Plan*, the work of the chief engineer, Francis J Forty.[6] In practice, however, the Second World War hastened the westward migration of the fashion wholesalers and showrooms to the area north of Oxford Street, which had already begun

2

3

1   Children's paddling pool (now turfed over),
    views south towards Cullum Welch House and
    Great Arthur House beyond, 1964

2   Aerial view of the Genuine Beer Brewery,
    Golden Lane, 1807

3   Map of London (detail) by R.ichard Horwood, 1795

in the 1930s. The LCC and Royal Fine Art Commission criticized Forty's plan as too conservative with its limited proposals for new roads and more open space, and in response the City brought in two well-respected architects, Charles Holden and William Holford, to make revisions.

The City of London Corporation had been the first public authority in England to build social housing, in the 1860s. Its policy by the twentieth century was to concentrate most of its housing activities in healthy suburban areas such as Camberwell and Sydenham Hill, encouraging the drift of population away from the Square Mile that coincidently made more space for business users. The City's population in 1851 was 130,000; by 1939 it was 9,000 and in 1951 it was 5,000, with only 48 people living in the worst-damaged ward of Cripplegate Without, the site of Barbican.[7] The corporation nevertheless recognized that some key workers such as caretakers, police officers and nurses needed to live centrally and, as well as building flats in the late 1940s and early 1950s on the Old Kent Road, it also sought a site within the City itself. Holden and Holford suggested the corporation buy and redevelop the remains of Bridgewater Square, just north of Beech Street, but the Ministry of Health rejected the proposal because the land was so expensive.[8]

The City of London Corporation's Public Health Committee turned its eyes towards cheaper land on the boundary with the working-class borough of Finsbury. Its chairman, Eric F Wilkins, was drawn to the derelict site off Golden Lane, where Finsbury Borough Council was slowly removing the rubble at the rate of 7,000 cubic yards (5,300 cubic metres) per month; such was the height of the mound that he estimated that it would take three years to clear.[9] The City acquired these 4.7 acres (1.9 hectares) of land (including No. 40 Fann Street) in February 1951, having already made an order for their development at 200 persons per acre, the maximum permitted under the *County of London Plan*. There then followed protracted negotiations with Finsbury, whose

councillors were anxious to secure some of the flats for their own tenants. The City saw its emphasis on small flats as not only suitable for its key workers, identified as mainly couples with small children or none, but also as a means of keeping out Finsbury's large working-class families; in November 1952 only 12.5 per cent of the initial nominations, or 42 flats, were offered to the borough, later increased to 55.[10] The City's surveyor produced a scheme for a single 9-storey slab, which the Common Council accepted in June 1950.[11] The LCC was also happy, but after discussions with the Royal Institute of British Architects (RIBA) in March 1951 the Public Health Committee determined to hold an open competition. Based on the surveyor's estimates, the committee prepared a brief for a mixture of small flats: 35 per cent with one bedroom, 45 per cent with two and 15 per cent with three; 5 per cent of the units were to be bedsitters. It preferred small 'working' kitchens to those combined with living-room accommodation, in a break from working-class traditions, but asked for private balconies large enough for a cot or pram to be provided in the larger dwellings. The conditions of the competition also gave a preference for staircase access to the flats rather than the long balconies found in most local authority housing, though they were not wholly precluded so long as they did not run past living rooms or bedrooms. Car parking, a laundry and drying areas were excluded as expensive and unnecessary, but the committee asked for a community centre and children's playground. It asked that the existing road pattern be disregarded but that the LCC's 100-foot height limit should be exceeded only in special circumstances. The flats were to be centrally heated, then still a novelty in public housing since few tenants could afford the additional charges.[12]

The first major housing competition since that held by Westminster City Council for Churchill Gardens in 1945, Golden Lane attracted 178 entries from across Britain, many by young architects. They were exhibited for a week in March 1952 at London's Guildhall. The Public

Health Committee reported that 'a large majority of the entries reach a high standard of design, many being valuable contributions to the study of urban housing'.[13]

Entries 172, 173 and 174 were by Peter Chamberlin (1919–78, known since schooldays as Joe after the politician), Geoffry Powell (1920–99) and Christoph Bon (1921–99). They had met at Kingston School of Art in 1948–9 when first Bon and later Powell joined Chamberlin as assistant teachers in the School of Architecture founded by the architect Eric Brown in 1941. Chamberlin, a conscientious objector in the war, had been among the first students to take the course; he stayed on to become Brown's deputy and a partner in his architectural practice, collaborating on exhibition work that included the 'Seaside' section of the Festival of Britain. Powell had studied at the Architectural Association as one of a cohort that also included Philip Powell (no relation) and Hidalgo Moya. The three had similarly moved on to work with their head of school, in their case as assistants to Frederick Gibberd, at the height of his reputation as a designer of flats and low-cost housing, with whom they developed a love of bright colour. The son of Swiss hoteliers, Bon had grown up in St Gallen and studied at Zurich's Federal Institute of Technology before gaining practical experience with Banfi, Belgiojoso, Peressutti and Rogers in Milan; he also worked briefly in London for Holford on his plan for the City. Another Swiss, Alfred Roth, introduced him to Brown, who invited him to teach at Kingston.

By 1951 the group was growing restless. Powell recalled that 'Eric Brown was a splendid person, but difficult to work with. … He complained that [we] didn't keep time, didn't wear the white coats expected of architectural assistants, and he thought we wanted to usurp his position.'[14] They resolved to set up their own practice and the Golden Lane competition provided an opportunity. Chamberlin, Powell and Bon (CPB) came up with three different solutions, and Powell suggested that if they submitted all three they would have a better chance of winning. That by

Bon was jointly credited with Chamberlin, who also produced his own design. The other two assistants, Charlie Greenberg and Roy Christy, did not enter, though Greenberg later worked on Barbican.

The RIBA nominated Donald McMorran as the competition's independent assessor, beginning a long association with the City as a designer of housing and police buildings in traditional styles.[15] Powell and Bon admired McMorran's work 'in its way', Bon describing it as 'post-modern before it had even started'. When Powell got his drawings in on the deadline of 31 January 1952 only by not completing the cross-hatching, the kindly McMorran finished them for him. Looking at the drawings today, this is hard to tell. [16] Powell was 31, relatively mature compared to Powell and Moya when they had won the competition for Churchill Gardens aged 24 and 25 respectively — housemates since student days, they had each drawn up their schemes on the same dining room table.

Two unplaced entries to the Golden Lane competition have long overshadowed the winning scheme. Both designed by recent graduates from King's College, Newcastle, these were proposals for long slabs with broad access 'promenades' or 'streets in the sky' — one by Jack Lynn and Gordon Ryder, and the other by Alison and Peter Smithson. Drawings only survive for the entry by the Smithsons. It is hard to imagine that they would have had the subtlety of the estate as finally built, or dealt so convincingly with the spaces and levels between the blocks. Chamberlin's independent scheme comprised a 19-storey block, with medium-rise slabs surrounded by a web of 2-storey terraces across the remaining site. Something of its character can be gleaned from CPB's later housing at Vanbrugh Park, Greenwich, although much of the detailed design there was by Powell.[17] What Bon's entry looked like is now unknown.

Geoffry Powell's scheme (figs. 4–5) was declared the winner on 26 February 1952, and thus was

4

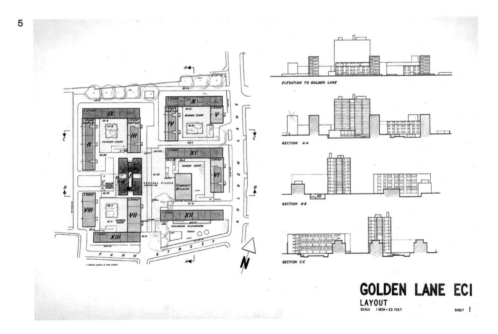

5

4, 5 Geoffry Powell's competition entry and winning design

born the partnership of Chamberlin, Powell and Bon. Monty Richards, clerk to the Public Health Committee, phoned to say he had won and to check if he was up to the job. Powell tried to reassure him. 'Of course we can' declared Chamberlin, the natural leader of the group characteristically coming to the fore.[18] The *Architects' Journal* declared CPB among its 'men of the year', 'for proving that three solutions stand more chance of winning a competition than one, and that a competition is still one of the classic ways of establishing a practice'.[19] Ove Arup and Partners were appointed the engineers.

Donald McMorran considered Powell's scheme economical, since much of it could be built of load-bearing brick, and he admired 'a village like character in the planning of the central piazza and "village hall"'.[20] It set the smallest flats in an 11-storey tower that just met the 100-foot height restriction, with larger flats and maisonettes in courtyards of 3 and 6-storey blocks around it. Powell strenuously limited views of the derelict wasteland all around the estate by facing the living rooms inwards, where he used the excavations left by the deep warehouse basements to create sunken gardens and to conceal community buildings and stores below the main walkways. As he explained at the time, 'The areas surrounding the Site offer no interesting outlook or views. An attempt therefore has been made to create interest within the site and the layout is inward looking in character.'[21] The central block provided an eye-catcher while closing vistas in the manner of the 'townscape' studies by Hubert de Cronin Hastings, Thomas Sharp and Gordon Cullen that had been published in *The Architectural Review* from the late 1940s. These developed a theme first explored in the writings of the nineteenth-century Austrian planner Camillo Sitte, whose work secured a timely translation into English in 1945 but was already known to Frederick Gibberd and his students. The same pattern of mixed development around internal squares had informed his Somerford Estate in Dalston, a lower-density mix of flats with some houses designed while Powell was in his office.

The Estate as Built

The principles behind Powell's design remained unaltered, though little else did. Now the work of three architects rather than one, their revised scheme responded to changing ideas and an easing in the regulations controlling the height of buildings. They made major revisions in 1952, when the layout was amended and the courtyards enlarged, and each block assumed an individual character and bolder scale. Further changes followed the start of work at the south-east corner of the site, rolling out northwards and westwards for nearly a decade. The design for the main part of the estate was finalized (while already well under construction) in April 1955. Work on the foundations to the first block, Bowater House, began in 1953, but old foundations, vaults and walls buried on the site caused delays, as did securing the freehold of the one occupied building on the site. Nevertheless, in July 1954 the lord mayor Sir Noël Vansittart Bowater Bt laid a foundation stone in the presence of Thomas Cuthbert Harrowing and Stanley Cohen, Wilkins's successors as chairmen of the Public Health Committee, who gave their names to the smallest blocks. Sir George Cullum Welch was lord mayor in 1957–8. Other blocks were named after streets previously on the site, save for Crescent House, simply named for its shape.

Each block gained a jaunty feature or twist, the *Architects' Journal* suggesting that the staircase at Bowater House was 'straight from the set of *West Side Story*'.[22] Powell recalled that Harrowing hated housing, and hated having to take the scheme through the LCC; Cohen was more supportive, except that he objected to the view of the central tower from his own flat on Moorgate. 'Can't you turn it round?' he asked, although the east–west direction was important in giving sunshine to every flat. The LCC planner Arthur Ling also started to turn round the blocks of the model submitted with the scheme for planning permission. For a later meeting, Powell firmly screwed down a revised version from underneath.[23] The greatest change was to the

6

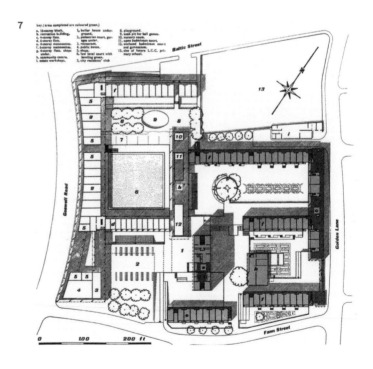

6 Geoffry Powell, Christoph Bon and Joe Chamberlin, 1953
7 Estate plan, 1957

tower, Great Arthur House, when in April 1955 it was raised to 15 and then 16 storeys; an early example of the LCC's more relaxed policy towards height controls, on its completion in 1957 it was briefly Britain's tallest residential block.

Like many authorities at the time, the City sought building materials thought not to require regular maintenance.[24] The maisonettes, largely detailed by Bon, have blue and dark red panels (fading in 2020) behind textured glass, their construction of load-bearing cross-walls faced in a pinkish brick clearly expressed. Wilkins and Harrowing were unhappy with the stairs in the maisonettes coming out of the living rooms, so Powell took them to see houses at Ealing with just this arrangement.[25] The open-tread concrete stairs (black terrazzo in Hatfield House) are wholly cantilevered to ensure that there is no wasted living space and little loss of light, creating a low sitting area below them (fig. 8), while large sliding staircase windows give interest to the elevations and much additional height and light elsewhere in the room. The stairs of the two-bedroom maisonettes on the top floors have bookshelves tucked underneath the treads, a clever use of space. Only in the largest three-bedroom top floor maisonettes are there timber stairs set in front of the kitchen (fig. 9).

Powell was primarily responsible for Stanley Cohen House and the community centre, later followed by the sports facilities and the public house. Stanley Cohen House, facing Golden Lane itself and kept relatively low so as not to block morning sunshine from the rest of the estate, had the greatest variety of accommodation, from bedsits to two-bedroom flats. Its pick-hammered concrete — the first use of the technique by the practice — was inspired by the 'Mining' section of 'The Land of Britain' complex at the Festival of Britain, designed as a dark pyramid by Michael Grice of the Architects' Co-Partnership. All these early blocks made a feature of Pilkington's opaque and wired glass, but bold paint colours were equally important, including black for Stanley Cohen House. After the estate was listed in 1998 the original colour scheme was restored

by the Corporation, advised by Frank Woods (a later partner in the firm) with Powell and Bon, Chamberlin having died in 1978.

Powell also took charge of the landscaping. Most striking was the use of the old basements to create different garden levels, with patterns of paving amid areas of grass and rose bushes, lawns and shallow pools crossed by stepping stones (fig. 16). The service road from Fann Street was a more important feature in the competition design than as built, but it was given emphasis by the terminal feature of a circular, raised bastion, introducing a circular counterpoint to the rectilinear housing blocks. It gives a hint of Powell's abiding interest in creating picturesque compositions by the most formal of means, though whether this was conceived as a medieval relic or an eighteenth-century garden feature he never revealed. The one specimen poplar tree, planted between Bayer and Basterfield houses, grew sideways and was removed.

Chamberlin took over responsibility for Great Arthur House (fig. 10–11), devising the curtain walling on the main facades from aluminium and Pilkington's speckled 'Muroglass' in golden yellow with vertical firewalls. This was replaced sympathetically in 2018–9. He later added a curved oversailing roof feature, concealing the lift mechanism, and two water tanks described as 'giant saucers' as a *jeu d'esprit*[26]. The 120 one bedroomed flats were neatly appointed, with built-in cupboards and a sliding screen so that the living and bedroom spaces could be partly opened up if required. For the inhabitants of the upper floors, Chamberlin laid out the roof with tubs of trees, a pergola and water garden (fig. 17). A later assistant at CPB, Greg Penoyre who worked on Barbican in the late 1970s, recalled going up there to eat his lunch after site visits, but in 1981 it was closed following a suicide.[27]

Two other commissions realized in 1954–7 repeated the brightly coloured curtain walling of Great Arthur House, Bousfield School and a seed factory at Witham, demolished in 1987, just ahead

8

9

8   Living room of a typical two-bedroom maisonette, 1956
9   Staircase of a three-bedroom top floor maisonette, 1958

10

11

10 Great Arthur House in construction, 1956
11 Drawing of Great Arthur House flat by Geoffry Powell
12 Perspective drawings by Christoph Bon, 1952

of the first post-war listings. Golden Lane, however, saw a transition in the style of CPB's work when, at the Ministry of Housing and Local Government's suggestion, the estate was extended to Baltic Street in November 1952 and in May 1954 to Goswell Road, making a total of 7 acres (2.8 hectares). Hatfield House repeated the style of Basterfield House, with an additional level of garden bedsits at the level of the sunken courtyard, and was then extended. Two further blocks were also designed with mainly very small flats. Cullum Welch House, in the pinkish brick used earlier, was a modern take on a Victorian warehouse; containing neat, square bedsits, it 'almost designed itself' according to one assistant, Michael Neylan.[28]

Crescent House (fig. 13) is a more complex double-depth block whose varied width is taken up in open galleries between two ranges of mainly small flats. The ground floor was taken up by shops to meet demands from the LCC. Mainly designed by himself and Neylan in 1954–5, Joe Chamberlin recalled difficulties in building at 200 ppa on a long narrow site where towers could not be considered; in return for keeping Crescent House low, he secured a 16th floor for Great Arthur House.[29] Neylan too felt that when they came subsequently to design the elevations of Crescent House, 'they were changing, like everyone, they were "searching" for a new way'.[30]

The aesthetic of Crescent House differs from that of the rest of the estate. Its pick-hammered concrete surfaces and the external expression of the vaulted ceilings on its top floor adopts much of the idiom of Le Corbusier's Maisons Jaoul, built in 1954–6 at Neuilly-sur-Seine outside Paris, and anticipates the style of the Barbican Centre, for which CPB made their first proposals in these years. Repeated lines of small shell vaults became a common feature of their designs in the late 1950s, well seen at Murray Edwards College (formerly New Hall) in Cambridge and in rooftop views of Barbican. Dr Anthony Flint of Flint and Neill, engineers with whom CPB were then working at Two Saints School, recalled that all the partners were young and enthusiastic about exploring new

solutions. They toured concrete construction and finishes in Norway with the Cement and Concrete Association around 1960, which may have influenced the final choice of finishes here.[31] The western side follows the line of Goswell Road, the curve giving an extra dynamic to the syncopation of the roof vaults. Ian Nairn described the effect as 'so complex that it defies description, and unlike most such attempts it does manage to achieve organic complexity, so that you feel that the result is right even if your intellect can't see why'.[32] Other materials are dark timber and mosaics, making for a more serious aesthetic than is found in the rest of the estate. The curve meant, too, that the block widens at its southern end, permitting an internal courtyard and some larger flats at this end. Powell recalled that a key document was the City's site plan showing the road boundaries; it was wrong and the building overhung Goswell Road by inches. So, he recalled, the City moved the road.[33]

Crescent House terminates in The Shakespeare public house (fig. 14) by Powell, who had designed a pub for his student thesis. Now completely remodelled, outside and in, it gives no indication of the quest for a modern interpretation of the traditional English pub considered so important in the 1940s and again in the 1960s, when a few large breweries with their own architects' departments came to dominate the industry.

The larger site made possible the elimination of a block north and west of Great Arthur House and the City Corporation agreed in September 1956 to foundations for a swimming pool to be built at a later date. It went ahead when the City rejected proposals for a pool at Barbican in June 1958 as too expensive, and was eventually realized by Powell in 1960–3 following an Act of Parliament.[34] As well as a 20-metre (66-feet) pool, the long, highly glazed range also featured a games hall, with a dark, sunken section at right angles containing a nursery with a playground on top. This included a rectangular paddling pool (fig. 1), whose stepping stones now sit in a sea of turf, as well as a sunken circular area for ball games. A plan of the estate as built was published in June 1957 (fig. 7).

south east court from Golden Lane

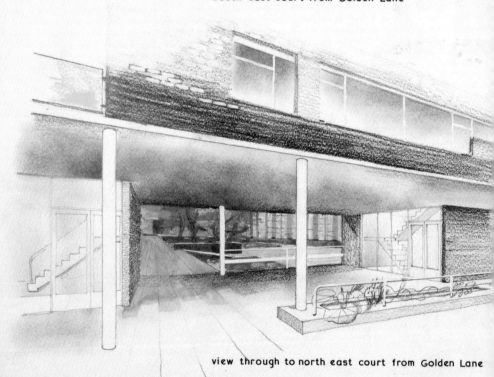

view through to north east court from Golden Lane

CHAMBERLIN
POWELL &
BON

GOLDEN LANE HOUSING

perspectives gp   21 july 52

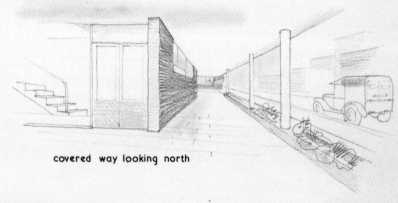

covered way looking north

13

14

13 View of Crescent House along Goswell Road, 1962
14 The Shakespeare public house, 1963

15

16

15 View into the estate from Golden Lane, as originally
built with an open collonade, 1958
16 View across the pond, towards Bayer House,
Stanley Cohen House is on the right, 1958

17 Great Arthur House roof garden, 1957

The Importance of Golden Lane

As completed in late 1962, the estate contained 1,400 dwellings, a swimming pool and badminton court, tennis courts (first planned as a bowling green), nursery and playground (including a paddling pool now turfed over), community centre and club room, and a line of shops with a public house facing Goswell Road. Golden Lane was fortunate, for with the City as a client and a high density, all its amenities could be built — Berthold Lubetkin had a very different experience in Finsbury where the reduced density of Priory Green made its communal facilities unviable.

Golden Lane can be seen as an eclectic first job, with Barbican charting the evolution over 30 years not only of a firm's career but also of post-war housing in general. Yet as a response for building at high densities at a time when tall flats were seen as opening up picturesque green space, most famously at Alton West where a real Capability Brown landscape was repurposed, it has a wider interest.

The spaces and the relationship between the blocks are as important as the actual buildings, so that the whole estate is a single piece of architecture like the quadrangles of the London's Inns of Court illustrated in the architects' 1959 report on Barbican.[35] Churchill Gardens, built to the same density, makes only a partial attempt at this, with its large, separated blocks and greater open space meaning that hard play areas and changes in level are limited and the experience less intense. Although both firms designed their own landscaping, CPB took the firmer hand. They believed that only strong, simple forms could survive, and that when looking down from the upper flats these would form part of the overall pattern of the estate. Even the roof of Great Arthur House was developed as a public space. In 1957 Powell claimed that 'there is no attempt at the informal in these courts. We regard the whole scheme as urban. We have no desire to make the project look like a garden suburb.'[38] The estate as finally built has all the *joie de vivre* of the picturesque movement, heightened by its contrasting shapes and colours. Yet its treatment of landscape is very different to that of its suburban contemporaries, rejecting the open greensward in favour of giving every piece of land a function. The landscape was registered Grade II in 2020, following the listing of the buildings in 1998 — 12 separate entries, with Crescent House listed Grade II* as the precursor for Barbican.

Many people do not know that Golden Lane exists. It is overshadowed by its massive neighbour, Barbican, for which CPB made preliminary proposals in 1955 and which was eventually built to their designs in 1963–82. Perhaps because it was a first job or perhaps because of the constraints on space, the flats were minutely planned to an exceptional degree and well appointed. They attracted many young professionals, including one architect as well as doctors, clergymen and married students. Paying the rent by cheque, as some of these tenants did, was newsworthy in 1958.[37] Yet it is a reminder of the rigid controls found in public housing in the 1950s that the architects could dare to suggest that the tenants hang the same curtain linings and nets to give a common appearance to the elevations of Great Arthur House. That proposal was ignored, but the tenants took pride in Golden Lane nevertheless, on-site management remained through the 1970s and 1980s, and there were never the social problems found in estates elsewhere. Well received by the architectural press at the time, the flats remained popular and have become still more so, attracting a range of residents although enjoying a particular cachet with architects and conservationists. The government introduced Right-to-Buy legislation in October 1980, and now half the flats are leased, an exceptionally high proportion for blocks of flats.

FOOTNOTES

1   Alan McLeod, https://abetterbeerblog427.com/2015/06/13/the-hillars-of-golden-lane-cripplesgate-without/, accessed 31 August 2020.

2   *The Builder*, vol.37, no.1884, 15 March 1879, p.291.

3   Simon Bradley and Nikolaus Pevsner, The Buildings of England, *London*, 1, *The City of London*, Harmondsworth, 1997, p.286.

4   Charles Holden and W G Holford, *The City of London, A Record of Destruction and Survival*, London, Architectural Press, 1951, p.184.

5   https://alondoninheritance.com/thebombedcity/hotwater-court-fann-street-golden-lane-estate/, accessed 31 August 2020.

6   J H Forshaw and Patrick Abercrombie, *The County of London Plan*, London, Macmillan, 1943, pp.24–5; Francis J Forty, *Report of the Improvements and Town Planning Committee on the Preliminary Draft Proposals for Post-War Reconstruction in the City of London*, London, Batsford, 1944.

7   Conditions for competition, Questions of Competitors and Answers thereto, is 4 September 1951, COL/CSD/HO/05/001, London Metropolitan Archives (LMA).

8   Corporation of London, *Reconstruction in the City of London*, Final Report to the Improvement and Town Planning Committee by Joint Consultants Charles Holden and W G Holford, 1947; Charles Holden and W G Holford, *The City of London, A Record of Destruction and Survival*, London, Architectural Press, 1951, p.85; COL/PD/71/13; London Metropolitan Archives.

9   Corporation of London, Public Health Committee, 6 February 1948, COL/CC/PBC/01/02/49, LMA.

10   Corporation of London, Public Health Committee Minutes, 25 November 1952, COL/CC/PBC/01/02/50; Barbican Committee Minutes, 25 September and 28 November 1960, COL/CC/BRD/01/01/001, LMA.

11   G7/12/20, LMA.

12   COL/CSD/HO/05/001, LMA.

13   Corporation of London, Public Health Committee Minutes, 26 February 1952, COL/CC/PBC/01/02/50, LMA.

14   Geoffry Powell in conversation, 6 January 1999.

15   Edward Denison, *McMorran and Whitby*, London, RIBA Publishing, 2009, pp.57–60; 102–13.

16   Christoph Bon and Geoffry Powell in conversation, 6 January 1999.

17   *Architects' Journal*, vol.115, no.2977, 20 March 1952, pp.358–62.

18   *The Times*, no.52257, 11 March 1952, p.10; Geoffry Powell in conversation, 6 January 1999.

19   *Architects' Journal*, vol.117, no.3020, 15 January 1953, p.72.

20   *Architects' Journal*, vol.115, no.2977, 20 March 1952, pp.354, 358–62.

21   COL/CSD/HO/05/001, p.6, LMA.

22   'Bowater House', *Architects' Journal*, vol.132, no.3428, 29 December 1960, pp.931–42 (p.932).

23   Geoffry Powell in conversation, 6 January 1999.

24   CLRO, B10f, 1714, LMA.

25   Corporation of London, Public Health Committee Minutes, 27 October 1952, COL/CC/PBC/01/02/50, LMA.

26   *Architects' Journal*, vol.125, no.3252, 27 June 1957, pp.947–8.

27   *Building Design*, no.2012, 4 May 2012, p.19.

28   Notes on CPB by Michael Neylan, March 2000, courtesy of Frank Woods.

29   Peter Chamberlin, 'Architects' Approach to Architecture', lecture notes, 4 February 1969.

30   Michael Neylan in conversation, 19 August 2005.

31   Dr Anthony Flint in conversation, 17 March 2006.

32   Ian Nairn, *Modern Buildings in London*, London Transport, 1964, p.4.

33   Geoffry Powell in conversation, 6 January 1999.

34   Corporation of London, Public Health Committee, 25 September 1956, COL/CC/PBC/01/02/052; Barbican Committee, 6 June 1958, 24 October 1960, COL/CC/BRD/01/01/001, LMA.

35   Chamberlin, Powell & Bon, *Report to the Court of Common Council of the Corporation of the City of London on residential development within the Barbican area* (London, CPB), April 1959, p.56.

36   Geoffry Powell, 'Golden Lane Housing Scheme', *Architectural Association Journal*, vol.72, no.811, April 1957, p.216.

37   *Architects' Journal*, vol.127, no.3281, 16 January 1958, pp.100–1.

38   *Architects' Journal*, vol.125, no.3252, 27 June 1957, p.947.

Joan Flannery

SO   What brought you to Golden Lane Estate?

JF   I was living in a small flat in Sutton Dwellings in Islington. It was the late 1960s, and I was on my own with a son, with nowhere for him to play outside. A delightful lady who taught me to swim, Mrs Ing, lived on Golden Lane Estate, and she suggested I apply to the council for a place there. A woman from the council came round to visit me at Sutton Dwellings, which only had two rooms. I'd decorated one of them with boys' things: a small wardrobe, some playthings and so on. She looked around and said, 'But where is your bedroom?' I replied, 'I sleep here, on the couch!' After about a year we managed to get a place on the estate. I wanted to wait for a vacancy on Golden Lane, as my son was at school at St Luke's by Old Street roundabout — which at that time was just a roundabout, there was no tube station. I was working nearby in Shoe Lane in Farringdon, and the fact that I was working in the City helped, I think. We moved into the estate in November 1969, and it was fantastic as there was central heating!

SO   Which block did you move to?

JF   We moved into Hatfield House, a maisonette with two bedrooms. My son had the bedroom overlooking the tennis courts, and I had the small one overlooking Baltic Street, which was a cold room, as it was north-facing. We were very happy there, and we were lucky as we had some good neighbours, but I always said that once my son was older, I would move to a smaller flat in Great Arthur House. When he went to university, it seemed like the right time to transfer — plus there was a £10 saving in rent!

SO   What was the estate like when you first moved there?

JF   In those days there was a woman, I don't know what her title would have been, but she was quite strict and went around the estate telling people their curtains were dirty and so on. There were all sorts of rules; you couldn't move in at weekends, for example, or after dark. We had a laundry room in the basement of Hatfield; in fact, each block had one of their own. It was like the Aussie soap opera Prisoner: Cell Block H — a lot of the action took place in the laundry.

so   Were there many families living here then?

JF   Yes, a lot. There was a lot of organized activities for children in the community centre, such as dancing classes for the girls, birthday parties, Father Christmas etc. Fewer women were going out to work back then, so there were more mothers at home who had time to organize such events.

so   You now own your flat in Great Arthur House. Did you buy it when the Right to Buy scheme came in?

JF   Not straight away, I didn't buy it until 1988. My friend, Ivy, who lived upstairs, bought hers in 1982, which I think was the first year you could. I didn't buy mine until I was retiring and received a lump sum which I used to purchase the flat. I had a great friend, Tom, who lived in Crescent House on the estate, and we were both worried about the NHS, and getting old. We decided that if we bought our flats, at least we would have something to sell to help us in our old age. Soon after I bought it, however, the estate boiler system packed up.

so   As a leaseholder, were you worried that more things were going to go wrong, and you would have to pay for them?

JF   I wasn't too worried. It meant I had to put my own heating in, for example, but this also meant I could choose where to put the radiators. In the tenants' flats, the council just boxed off the original space and hung the radiators in front. Being a leaseholder meant I could say 'I want this' or 'I want that', whereas tenants didn't get the choice.

so   Do you know how many are tenants and how many are leaseholders in Great Arthur House?

JF   I don't know what the split is at the moment, but initially there were 42 leaseholders out of 120 flats. But of course, some of the original ones have died. In fact, I can't think of anyone apart from myself now.

so   Did you know a lot of the people in the block when you first moved here?

JF   I knew some of the people because I was involved in the residents' association, which almost became a full-time job. First, I was the secretary, then became chairman. I used to go to the housing committees, too; it was all quite time-consuming. The association was very active then. Tom was originally part of the tenants' association, and I the owners' association, and between us, we covered the whole of the estate with information.

SO   Do you think that community spirit changed over the years?

JF   After the Right to Buy scheme came in, and people bought their homes, I think there should have been a policy to say that if you wanted to sell your flat or house, you should have to sell it back to the council. Unfortunately, that didn't happen, and what you get now is absentee landlords. There are a lot of people here who work in the City and sleep here, but they are not involved in the community. Families with young children are better. You seem to get families in waves. All the children grow up, and then comes the next wave. But no, it's not the same as it was. It really isn't. I think Margaret Thatcher thought people would buy and then hand their homes down to their kids, but people move so much these days.

SO   Was it always a desirable place to live?

JF   Oh, yes. When I worked for BT, I helped with an adventure playground up the road, just behind St Luke's church. I managed to get telegraph poles, and that sort of thing for it. One weekend somebody set fire to the playground, and people would say to me, 'It's alright for you, living in the posh flats'.

SO   Has the estate changed much physically, over the years?

JF   It was more open, but people used to cut through the estate at night, and the residents used to complain that some people were using it as a pissoir. So we installed gates between Bayer House and Stanley Cohen House so that we could close it off at night.

SO   Do you mean the brick infill on Golden Lane?

JF   No, that was nothing to do with us. I don't know whose idea that was. I mean the small gate on the corner that we could lock. But it took five years for the council to do that, the City of London is so slow! I also desperately tried to get more ramps. By Crescent and Cullum Welch, for example, there are two little steps, which doesn't seem much, but if you have a walker, or a trolley or baby in a buggy—it's a problem. But my proposal got stopped, and the best I managed to get there was a handrail.

'You seem to get families in waves.'

SO And what about the sports facilities on the estate, such as the tennis courts and the swimming pool — did you use them?

JF My son used the swimming pool, but only for a short while because he said it was too small and too warm. But he did learn to swim there, that's where Mrs Ing had her classes.

SO Do you ever think about moving out of London and being closer to your son?

JF Well, I would need a car. And I don't drive, and there are no buses. It's lovely where he lives, but his road doesn't even have a name! There's not even a shop there — the post office is only open Thursday afternoons. I like to at least be able to nip out and buy a packet of cigarettes.

SO And do you still get about on buses in London?

JF Not anymore, I have trouble with my circulation. I go down to the community centre with my walker on Tuesday afternoons where there's a 'memories club', it's only across the way so I can manage that. On the second Thursday of the month, we have what is called Read and Relax in the Ralph Perring Club, by the swimming pool and it's super — I really enjoy it. Alison, who lives downstairs, collects me. We go down to the first floor, she takes my walker down the stairs, and I just about manage to hang on to the railings; otherwise, you've got to go out the front door, up the slope and you still have three steps to go up.

SO I guess people don't think about steps until they are a problem. And what about living in a high-rise, has that been harder as you have got older?

JF No, not at all, as long as the lifts work. I love being up here and being able to see the sky.

SO Did you used to go to the rooftop of Great Arthur House?

JF I was living here for six years before I even found out there was a roof garden. In 1957, when the estate was built, there was no Barbican to look down on you. There weren't as many cars as there are now, so there was less pollution. Now it's too dirty and windy. The residents on the 15th floor, at the top, weren't pleased about people running about on the rooftop above them. There were also problems with the pond leaking. So now it's just opened once or twice a year for special occasions.

'I love being up here and being able to see the sky.'

SO The whole of the glass curtain walling was replaced in Great Arthur House recently wasn't it?

JF That's right. The new double-glazed windows have made it warmer, but I didn't suffer in the first place, as my flat is in the middle, so it's well insulated.

SO Now the estate is coming up to 60 years old, does your flat still work for you?

JF Yes. I find it interesting how people have changed their flats, but I've kept mine mostly original. I've adapted the kitchen a little, but largely it's as it was. Modern kitchen cupboards have wasted space above them, whereas here they are much more practical as they go all the way to the ceiling. There's a little square hatch, between the kitchen and the living room, and some people have blocked it off or shoved a TV in there, but I just love it.

Liz Davis, Fred Scott and Stella Scott

SO   How did you come to live on Golden Lane Estate?

LD   We used to live in Vauxhall and had a bad neighbour living below us. She wouldn't let us make any noise, and even complained if we were walking across the floor. We had to move. Fred initially went to see places in the Barbican but found that although the prices of the flats were manageable, the service charges were far too expensive. He was familiar with Golden Lane as he had worked with students on projects about the estate when he was teaching at the Architectural Association and at Kingston University.

SO   How long ago was that?

SS   Well I'm 35 now, and I think I was 12 when we moved here, so around 1998.

LD   So Fred came over to look at the flat we now live in. It had been empty for a while, it's impossible to imagine now, but at the time they couldn't sell it. Nobody wanted it because it was ex-council.

SO   That seems unbelievable now that the flats are so expensive and desirable, and just 23 years ago it was so different.

LD   It was a lot more 'council' back then, so it was different, but it was still an incredibly peaceful and wonderful place to live.

SS   The thing that I remember when we first moved here was all the net curtains. The original community slowly moved out, and within 10 or 15 years, more and more people had bought their maisonettes, and I noticed all the curtains came down.

LD   Yes, initially, when people started buying their flats through the Right-to-Buy scheme, it was affordable. But then when they became very expensive, even if you could get a 50 per cent discount, it wasn't feasible.

SO   Did you buy your flat from someone who had bought it through the Right to Buy?

LD Yes, he was a police officer.

SO Did the estate have a good reputation when you moved here?

SS Yes, it was a quiet estate. It was very community-driven. When we moved here, I was almost a teenager and moving from Vauxhall—it felt like we were moving to the countryside. I remember my friends coming to visit me to help strip the wallpaper off the walls, and they thought I'd moved to the back end of nowhere. Little did I know that we had actually moved more central. But compared to Vauxhall, which was noisy and full of chaos, where everyone would be out playing on the street, Golden Lane felt eerily quiet.

SO Did you know anybody that already lived on the estate?

LD No, but we quickly got to know our neighbours, who still live here. And Stella got very friendly with their daughter. And we soon met Joan Flannery, who pretty much ran the estate through the residents' association.

SO Did you get involved in the residents' association?

LD In the early days, Fred would go to quite a lot of the meetings in the community centre.

FS Yes, and I would go to the bar downstairs sometimes too, as you could get cheap drinks there. It attracted the older, original community. They would have bingo nights and that sort of thing.

LD I think they were annoyed about the new people who had bought flats and were moving into the estate. They were very welcoming to anyone from the nearby Peabody estate, but if they recognized you weren't a tenant, they were less friendly.

SO Was there that kind of division between council tenants and owners across the estate?

LD No, not at all. It was just a core group of people who used to go to the old bar. They were a faithful crowd that used to go there right until the end when it closed down, a few years ago. And I understand it. They must have thought, 'Who are all these people coming in?' The people who ran the bar were also responsible for renting out the community space above it, and to make it financially profitable, so they built another little bar in the corner of the community centre and

'It felt like moving to the countryside.'

got rid of all the wonderful original Ercol furniture that was in there.

FS Yes, there was a skip full of Ercol chairs! We told the estate office and thank goodness they managed to save them. They are now in the Ralph Perring club.

LD In 2015, there was a campaign to regenerate the community hall and turn it into a more useable space for the community, for all the different generations, and the people who ran the bar lost their fight to keep it. But times had changed. They were from a generation when people used to go to the pub every day, but people weren't doing that anymore. They were staying in watching TV at home and having a glass of wine. Now it is much more inclusive, and it's very successful.

SO What else has changed since you moved here?

SS There wasn't much to do here. Whitecross Street, which is now busy and vibrant with a food market, was completely dead. It was all boarded up during the week. Rumour has it that East London gangsters owned most of the street, and the council spent ten years taking them to court to get all the shops open. It was very old fashioned, and there were signs and posters from the 1960s. There was one place you could get cheap CDs and a good video store at the end. There were a few restaurants in the area like an Indian takeaway, an Italian and a vegetarian place. And that was about it. For a treat, we would go to the Pizza Express in the Barbican, above London Wall.

SO Were there other architects living on the estate at that time?

'The City of London wanted to fill in the pond with concrete.'

LD There was one other architect, who is still here now, he moved in at around the same time as us, and a few more by the time the Listed Building Guidelines for the estate were drawn up around 2005. The architect John Allan, who wrote the book on Berthold Lubetkin, worked on them, along with Fred and a few of the others. Some of them were quite strict about how the estate should look. They were purists; in fact, they used a picture of the blue plant pot we have in the garden as an example of what not to do with the outside space! But then again, there was the time when the City of London wanted to fill in the pond with concrete, so we needed proper guidelines.

SO Why did they want to fill it in?

FS The pond has these large square stepping stones that

kids love to jump from one to the other, and they said it was too dangerous.

ss   When my brother was living in the maisonette with his family, their kids would spend hours every summer, jumping back and forth, until they could do it absolutely perfectly.

so   How have the outside spaces changed since you've been here?

LD   It's become a lot greener. And that's what Chamberlin, Powell and Bon intended.

ss   The pond goes through different periods. At the moment it's quite deserted, but I remember there was a time when it was like an oasis—full of reeds, fish, waterlilies. There was this huge white carp we called Moby Dick. He was there for at least 17 years.

FS   He had a cockney accent!

ss   And there was also a heron that would regularly come and land on the pond.

so   Has there been much of a change in your neighbours over the years?

LD   There's been an enormous change in the last few years which I think is due to Brexit. There were a lot of young families who bought here because of all the outside space, young professionals, designers etc., but they all left when the EU referendum happened. It's completely changed, now there are no kids out there at all.

so   How practical do you think the maisonettes are for families?

LD   Oh, totally, especially if you live on the ground floor like us.

ss   But not so great for teenagers. Buffy [Liz Davis] and I used to argue so much. We would have blazing rows. But the bedrooms have good locks on them, so that was good!

LD   Yes, I think it was tough for Stella when she was a teenager. In a 'normal house', you would have your own room to play music, make noise and that sort of thing with a bit of privacy. But here the bedrooms don't feel very private.

ss   The maisonettes are so open, there's nowhere to hide. Everything about the flat, in fact, the estate, is very exposed.

'There was this huge white carp we called Moby Dick.'

38

So as a teenager, it wasn't easy, but then again, I was living in central London. I had Old Street with all of its bars just a five minutes walk away. And there were places on the estate I could escape to — the best was the top of Great Arthur House.

SO   Did you manage to get onto the roof terrace?

SS   Yes, you used to be able to trick the lift doors by keeping them open, and it would default to the roof. I used to go up there with my friends after clubbing and look at the sunrise and watch the whole of London wake up.

SO   Are there any teenagers living on the estate now?

SS   You don't see many teenagers hanging out here, not like other estates. People look out of their windows, so there's never an opportunity for anyone to gather and be anti-social, and if they did, someone would complain straight away.

SO   Did you appreciate how lucky you were, living so centrally?

SS   Absolutely, you can walk to anywhere from here, and that was brilliant. You can walk to the river, or Dalston or Soho. When I used to go out clubbing, all my friends used to have to get the night bus home at the end of the night, and I would be able to walk home. I would go through High Holborn and Smithfield market and be in bed in 20 minutes. It was an absolute luxury, and my friends started to cotton on to it and come and stay over.

SO   And what about now, Buffy, does the flat still work for you?

LD   Yes. Fred has been quite ill and stays in most of the day, but I can go out through the door in the living room, and I am in the garden. I'm there from 8 am until 5 pm. Having the outdoor space, especially on the ground floor, you meet everybody that lives on the estate and someone will always stop by and have a chat. This flat has saved me. I couldn't have managed anywhere else.

In conversation   Pauline Mazzella

SO   What brought you to live on Golden Lane Estate?

PM   I've been a nurse since I was 17, and in 1999 when I was
about 30, I got a job at St Bart's hospital, which is nearby in
Smithfield, and they offered me a studio flat on the estate.
The Corporation of London owns it, but I'm a tenant through
the hospital. I've been here ever since — I wouldn't want to
be anywhere else.

SO   Do you remember what you thought about the flat when
you first saw it?

PM   I had been living in a two-bedroom flat, so when I first came
to see it, I thought it was a bit small, but it would do me for
a year. I was worried it was too close to work, and if people
knew I lived around the corner, it would be too easy for them
to call me and say, 'So and so is off sick, can you cover'.
I planned to live here for a year, to save some money and
then move on.

SO   You're not originally from London, are you?

PM   No, I was brought up in the North East, and I trained to be
a nurse in Hartlepool. I was about to get married when I
qualified. I thought I was going to have a perfect life with
the perfect husband, perfect job, perfect children. However,
I soon discovered my fiancé expected me to leave work
the day we got married and never to work again. But I was
an independent female, and that wasn't going to happen.
I thought okay, that's fine. I'll go to London.

SO   Were you familiar with the area around Golden Lane?

PM   Not at all. When I was first in London, I worked in
Hammersmith. I knew the Angel a little bit, but I had no
idea about the area and the Barbican, or the history of
Smithfield and St Bart's hospital. I spent the first year that
I lived here just walking around and getting to know it.

41   **SO**   Has the area changed much since then?

PM There's a lot more activity in the week, but at the weekend it is still quiet. Initially, the only open pub at the weekend was The Shakespeare, downstairs. If you go a bit further, to Clerkenwell, for example, it's much busier. But this area has remained very similar.

SO You mentioned you thought the flat was quite small when you first saw it, so now you've been here over 20 years, how have you made it work?

PM I now think it's perfect. I have a lot of stuff, but there is plenty of storage built into the flats. If I was allowed, however, I would knock the walls down and open up the kitchen, I'd make the bathroom an en-suite and reconfigure it a bit. There's a lot you could do with it, but it's lovely to live in as it is: it's light and airy.

SO Have you found it easy to get to know your neighbours?

PM Yes, really easy. I know everybody around my end of the block — once you get to the lifts, less so. I think most of us have lived here for a long time. There's an interesting mix of people. We had a lady directly opposite who, if she didn't like you, would let you know. She had a Zimmer frame that she'd try and hit you with when walking past — she was feisty! But luckily she liked me. Then there's another guy who also works at St Bart's. I used to know the man next door to me quite well, but then he sold his flat, and then it sold again, and ever since there have been various tenants moving in and out, but that's the exception. Everyone else seems to stay for a while. I don't think there are many council tenants left.

SO Do you get involved in any of the community activities on the estate?

PM Not really. I now have a full-time job working at The Royal London Hospital and I work long days. I used to do nights as well, so I don't really have time.

SO Do you like living on an estate, and what do you think of the architecture?

PM I do. I love the fact that there are different buildings, and each one is a different shape or colour, with a different personality. Over the years I've given them characters and names — like the tower in the middle, I call that The Giant. I came across a film on YouTube one day, a short video about an old lady who dances in the rain. During the downpour, there were people taking shelter under buildings, and as I was watching,

'I love the fact that there are different buildings, and each one is a different shape or colour, with a different personality.'

I realized that's where I live! I love the fact that people want to make films here. It feels special. They made a Jason Bourne movie here one year. I have no idea which part of the film it is, but I watch it, again and again, just so that I might see it.

SO   Do you think the estate is managed well?

PM   From my point of view, and my experience, the management has been fine. I've had a couple of episodes where I lost electricity for five days, and the estate office was very accommodating and helpful. I haven't run into any trouble with them. I think, as with anywhere, there are politics. Now and again you'll get a newsletter saying such and such has moved on, and this person has taken over. And of course, there was 'plantgate'.

SO   What was 'plantgate'?

PM   It was terrible. One of the things I love about the place is that it's beautiful in the summer — especially Crescent House where I live. When you walk up the steps, and you see everyone's outdoor pot plants, it feels like a Mediterranean courtyard. On the third floor, however, some of the plants had got a little overgrown. Instead of sensitively working with the residents to strip them back a bit, the estate office decided to go in heavy-handed and remove everything. It got very heated, and it caused a lot of stress and upset among the residents.

SO   Was it a fire safety issue following what happened at Grenfell Tower in 2017?

PM   I'm not sure. My feeling was that there was somebody new in management, and it seemed to coincide with that. After that incident, we were only allowed to have four pot plants outside our doors. I think they lacked an understanding of what it means to be part of the Golden Lane Estate community. It might work for things to be uniform and regimented on other estates, but here that doesn't work at all. You just have to look at the different buildings to realize some people have balconies and others have gardens, and we all use the outdoor space differently. When I first came here, in the first few years, there used to be a competition every July for who had the best plants. It was great. The judges would come round, and everybody would tidy up because it was judging time. That works much better than telling people, 'You have too many plants, get rid of them, it's a fire hazard'. Golden Lane isn't the same as most blocks of flats; you have to be a certain type of person to

'It feels like a Mediterranean courtyard.'

live here because we are all on top of each other, and the flats are compact. Even the maisonettes are relatively small.

SO Does it feel like you are all living on top of each other?

PM I quite like a bit of noise because it's identifiable noise, so it doesn't bother me. A few years ago, a couple living in a flat over in the corner of the block, above The Shakespeare pub, had a significant problem with noise coming from it. They got together with other flat owners to lobby the pub to install soundproofing. As my flat is close to the pub, I was invited to one of the meetings to discuss it one night. I spoke up and said, 'We all moved here knowing there's a pub underneath us. So we need to expect a certain amount of noise', and that didn't go down well! Personally, I like the familiarity of the noise, and knowing there are people downstairs having a good time is comforting.

SO Your flat is right on the Goswell Road, which is quite a busy and noisy road—is it a problem?

PM It means I can't have my windows open at the front, as the traffic is too noisy, and it's too dusty, but that's okay.

SO Do you use the parade of shops under Crescent House?

PM I do, I'm very good at using them. There's a good mix of shops. There's a hardware store run by a family that has been there for years. The mother rules the roost, she's a little dot of a person, and her sons are all big men—they're a delightful bunch of people. Although sometimes they can be a bit scary. You have to know exactly what you're asking for, as otherwise, they give you a certain look and presume you don't know anything because you're a woman. But generally, they are helpful. There's also an optician that has changed hands, but I have been going there for 20 years. It's a lovely independent shop. And there are three cafes, but the People's Choice, on the corner, is my favourite.

SO What about the other facilities on the estate, do you use them?

PM I use the swimming pool. I did once join the gym, but I hardly went. I used to try and go to the aerobics classes, but it's difficult as I am always at work. Now I tend to go to the pool just for a few laps. I'm not a very good or a fast swimmer, but it's just good to go there and be sociable. I tend to go in the afternoon in the week when I'm not working, and it's generally an older crowd that go, which I like.

SO What are the best things about living here?

PM The location is fantastic. It's really easy for me to get to work. Cheapside is just a ten-minute walk away, where there are shops, cafes, restaurants, and St Paul's Cathedral of course. Then there's Millennium Bridge that goes across to the Tate gallery. I can walk to the Barbican and sit in the gardens where there are the fountains and a lovely cafe. It's a fantastic place to live.

In conversation   Alan Lam and Yanki Lee

SO   I remember first meeting you around 2005, at the back of the parade of shops under Crescent House. You were in the middle of renovating your unit: how did you come to rent a shop on the estate?

AL   We came to know about the unit in 2004. Fred Scott and a few other residents had put together a temporary exhibition about the estate called 'Golden Lane Expo' in the vacant shop. We came to see it, and it made us intrigued about finding out more about it. When the exhibition finished, the unit became vacant, and we saw it advertised by a local estate agent. We decided to put together a simple proposal for the shop, and after a few rejected offers, we finally got it. And then we panicked!

SO   What were your plans for the shop?

AL   We have a lot of friends who are designers, and in the beginning, we thought it would be a shop selling furniture, products, accessories, that sort of thing. That was the starting point, but soon afterwards we began to think about how to use the space more creatively, and for it to be more than just a shop. We wanted to involve artists and the community. For us, that was much more rewarding than just running a shop.

YL   We had the concept of calling it 'Exhibit' from the beginning, and that was a solid foundation, and everything grew from there. Exhibit, as a word, is an action, rather than something static. The concept was to have something that was continually changing.

SO   What were your backgrounds before this?

YL   We are both from a design background. I came to London in 1998 to study at the Royal College of Art.

AL   I studied architecture in Hong Kong, and then in 2000, I came over to join Yanki in London. I was lucky to find a job relatively quickly, so I could financially support Exhibit.

'It's south-facing
and looks
onto the open
space and trees.'

SO What attracted you to Golden Lane Estate?

YL I grew up in Hong Kong, watching a lot of movies about London. The films portrayed the city as being gritty and rough. When I started at the RCA, which is in the wealthy area of Kensington, I was disappointed — it wasn't the London I was expecting. While studying, I worked on a project based in Shoreditch and Hackney, and that's when I decided I wanted to be closer to East London. We chose to live on Golden Lane Estate because of its design and the architecture, and a few friends from the RCA were moving here. Also, Alan's work was literally opposite the estate.

AL Every time I went out for lunch, I would walk through it and think, 'If I could find a place to live here, it would just be perfect!'

SO And what year was that?

AL It was 2002. Initially, we lived in a one-bedroom flat in Great Arthur House. A year later, Yanki went back to Hong Kong to do her Ph.D, and I decided to downsize to a studio. I've been there ever since — the landlords are very nice people.

SO In which block is the studio flat?

AL It's in Cullum Welch House, on the third floor, with a huge window at one end, which is very luxurious compared to Hong Kong standards. It's south-facing and looks onto the open space and trees. It has a lot of great qualities to it. It's small, measuring around 30 square metres, but because it's just me living there now, it's okay. We have rearranged the furniture about six or seven times over the years, to try and work out the best configuration — from very minimal to quite busy. In the end, we found the most comfortable was pretty much the same as when I first moved there: just a simple bed, a sofa and a regular dining table.

SO Do you think the size and design of the flats dictates how you live in them?

AL I don't think so. Because it is a simple rectangular shape, without awkward corners, it actually gives you more opportunity to try different things.

SO How does the estate, and the flats, compare to where you grew up in Hong Kong?

48

AL There are similarities. My parents own a flat that was built in the 1970s, so again, purpose-built with no awkward corners. But during the property boom in Hong Kong, smaller and smaller apartments were built for maximum profit. In comparison, the flats in Golden Lane are a much more generous size. The interiors of the flats in Hong Kong feel dictated. You have to put a sofa here, and a table there. There's no flexibility. It's as if the flats are designed for the furniture, as opposed to people. The same thing is happening in London now, with new apartment blocks. Property is unaffordable, and people are so desperate to own something, developers are building smaller and smaller apartments, and the quality is not there, not like it is in Golden Lane Estate.

SO   Tell me more about the exhibitions you curated for Exhibit, which involved the estate.

AL   After a couple of years of having the space, we decided to scale back the retail element of it. We curated a few projects with a direct link to the estate. For example, we invited RCA students to design objects and products that responded to Golden Lane Estate. In 2009, however, we decided to be more ambitious and devote the whole space to nine projects across 18 months, celebrating the 50th anniversary of the estate.

YL   We called it the 'Super Estates Project' and invited artists from around the world. When people think about social housing, they often have stereotypical views of run-down estates, with anti-social behaviour etc., but we don't have any of those problems here. The artists embraced the brief and appreciated the uniqueness of Golden Lane.
      They responded in very different ways. Some were very optimistic; others were humorous. One of the artists in residence was Katharina Lackner from Austria. When she first visited the estate, she noticed a lot of signs, such as 'No ballgames, no photography, no cycling'. No, no, no, no! She responded to the brief by breaking the rules and creating a sense of anarchy. She organized a paper plane throwing event with hundreds of white paper planes. We were worried the estate management would be against it because it would cause litter, or it might hit people and so on. But fortunately, they were very supportive of the whole Super Estates project.

'We called it the "Super Estates Project" and invited artists from around the world.'

SO   How did the Golden Lane residents respond to the project?

AL   We had a lot of interest from residents. Before we launched the project, we held an exhibition about Golden Lane and

AL   gathered a lot of archive material. That brought a lot of the residents into the gallery, and it was a good way of introducing the project. It was at the same time that the estate won an award, so there was generally a lot more interest in it and in modernism.

SO   Did the exhibition space evolve again once the Super Estates Project finished?

AL   To be honest when it finished, I lost a bit of steam. Yes, we celebrated the estate, but I thought, what next? I was hoping it would be the beginning of something, but it didn't answer any of the big questions. It wasn't a solution to the housing crisis or a way to improve living standards. We demonstrated to the public successful social housing, but Golden Lane Estate was created in unique circumstances after the Second World War when there was an opportunity to rebuild the City. That aspiration to build good social housing hasn't continued, so after the project, I felt deflated.

YL   We never really signed up for it to be a sustainable business. We wanted to do something for the estate and the community that felt important. We did a project called 'Golden Oldies', where I worked with a photographer and writer who were residents of Golden Lane. Together we interviewed and photographed a lot of the original residents, and that was wonderful. They spoke so optimistically about when they first moved here. Old Tom Williams, for example, used to be a postman and he moved into Crescent House with just a single chair. But he was so happy because it was the first time he had central heating and an indoor toilet. That sense of home and belonging was very important to the original residents. That project is now ten years old, and sadly most of them have passed away now. Through Exhibit, we helped establish something on the estate, and we are very proud of that.

SO   What do you think it is about Golden Lane Estate that makes it so successful?

AL   I think it was very clever to use the bombed landscape to create different levels. The fact that there are public and private zones, there's openness, but it doesn't compromise your privacy. I think the architectural layout is still very successful, but in terms of the community, that is changing. I've been living here for a long time now, and I've witnessed younger people moving in, and a lot of the older residents have gone. The original residents were much more open and friendly, and I think the people who are moving in now

'We wanted to do something for the estate and the community that felt important.'

are more introverted. It's not necessarily changing for the bad, but I can see a transition.

SO   What about the other shopkeepers; are they engaged with the Golden Lane Estate community?

AL   I don't think the other shops are that engaged with it. The units are double aspect, so there are two entrances: one facing the main street, and one at the back that opens out to the estate. But nobody has these open, which is understandable as there's not much footfall at the back.

SO   Has there been much of a change of ownership in the shops?

AL   Not too much. The cafe on the corner has changed hands since I've been here. They do very well, and there's always a constant queue of builders. There used to be John who ran the greengrocers. His father started the business, but he recently retired, and an Indian family now run it. There used to be a convenience store next door, and that's now a dentist. And then there's the hardware store, of course, that's been there a long time.

SO   What did your shop used to be?

AL   Originally, it was a butcher. At the very beginning, the shops were all the basics you might need: a butcher, a hairdresser, a greengrocer etc. In the lease, it states that you cannot cause competition among the other shops in the parade. Retail is changing though, and I think in ten years, these shops will be very different.

'I think in ten years, these shops will be very different.'

Bev Bytheway

SO How long have you lived on Golden Lane Estate?

BB I've been here around 14 or 15 years. I moved down from Manchester gradually. I was travelling between the two cities for a while, and then eventually London and Golden Lane Estate won over.

SO Why did you decide to buy a flat on the estate?

BB I used to be involved in an organization called New Contemporaries, which held annual touring exhibitions of emerging artists. I used to run the programme from my base in Manchester. For three consecutive years, we exhibited in the Barbican Curve Gallery. I needed a base when I was here, and I used to stay in a hotel across the road from the estate. I used to walk through it and spent a lot of time looking around it, so I got to know it. I also kept hearing about what a great place it was. In a rather abstract way, I thought if ever I were to move to London, this was the area I'd like to move to. One year when we were hanging the exhibition in the Barbican Curve, they had to do some renovations to the space, and they closed the gallery. I decided to go around to the local estate agents, and it just so happened that somebody was selling their maisonette at that time. I came to look at it, and I instantly fell for it.

SO Had you been inside any of the maisonettes before?

BB No, never! I'd looked through some windows but had never been inside them. A colleague of mine lived in Lillington Gardens in Pimlico, an estate by Darbourne and Darke. I often stayed with her when I was visiting London. It's a similar estate in a way, with lots of open garden spaces and public spaces—different architecture, but a similar concept. Maybe that influenced me because I was instantly smitten with the flat as soon as I walked through the door. I thought, 'Oh dear, I'm now going to have to find the money for this'. Up until then, it had been a bit of a fantasy.

SO What made it so special?

BB   I think it felt special partly due to the direct access to the garden. I had never lived in a flat with outdoor space before, and the fact that my living room door leads directly to the communal garden was a big attraction. It had an incredible sense of space and light — I thought it was just magic. It was an instant love affair with the flat and the estate.

SO   When you moved in, did you know anybody who lived here already?

BB   That's an odd story actually. When I came to London to pick up the keys for the flat, I was waiting for the estate agent to deliver them. I was excited as it was going to be my first weekend here. It was late March — I remember that as it was around my birthday — and as I was stood outside it started snowing, and a lady from further along the block came out in her slippers and walked past me. I looked at her, and she looked at me, and she said, 'Oh my god, it's Beverly Bytheway!' And I said, 'Oh my god, it's Jane Beckett!' Jane was my lecturer at university from decades ago, and she had completely changed my life. I had no idea she lived here. She asked me what I was doing, and I told her I was waiting for the keys for my new flat, and she said she had just moved into number 7. It was remarkable, but it's that kind of place. It seemed as if everybody I had ever known lived here. It was bizarre. I guess people come to live here because of the design and the architecture, and we have that in common.

SO   Do you think the architecture helps forge a community?

BB   I think the architecture has a lot to do with it. In the neighbouring Barbican Estate, for example, it's very internal. You have vistas across the estate, but you don't often see your neighbour. In Golden Lane, you are very aware of being part of something. There are layers and layers of glass in the flats, which create visibility. I can sit in my living room and see through to all the corners of the estate. You become familiar with the people who live here, as you see them every day. During the post-war years, when the estate was built, architects such as Chamberlin, Powell and Bon sought to foster communities that had been ripped apart during the war; and to build housing that was fit for the future. There was a sense of optimism, and there is still that community spirit today.

SO   I was reading the original competition brief for the estate, and the community centre was a significant part of the project. Is it still a central part of the estate?

'I can sit in my living room and see through to all the corners of the estate.'

BB It has recently been restored and renovated, and it's now running in a very different way than before. The initiative was resident-led, with a vigorous campaign to get it back into the heart of community life. There were lots of public meetings, consultations and ideas for what the centre could be, and how best to run it in the future. A residents' committee was formed and worked in partnership with the City of London. They were involved in the spec and the brief for Studio Partington, the architects who worked on the renovation. It's now a beautiful space — much more open and inclusive. There are all sorts of activities for different generations such as yoga, book readings, the hugely successful memory club, and the market days, of course.

SO Tell me more about the market days.

BB We held the first market day ten years ago. There were several different residents' groups on the estate, and we decided to all get together. There was a group called Golden Lane Record, who looked at creative ways of recording and documenting an archive of the oral history of the estate. There was the gardening group, and also Exhibit — the gallery space on Goswell Road. Because we all live in compact flats, we came up with the great idea of a market day to recycle and sell some of our things. We leafleted the whole estate and offered residents a stall to sell whatever they liked. That first year we had it under the Crescent House, at the back of the shops, because it is under cover. There was a fantastic response — and we had 20 or 25 stallholders selling all kinds of things. There was a wonderful young couple selling homemade bread, and someone was selling vintage cameras. It was a great day. From then on, it became a yearly event, which I organize. I try and get some of the artists and the makers that live on the estate to get involved.

SO As well as the market days, you started the allotment group, didn't you?

BB Yes, that was around the same time. There was a funding stream set up by the Mayor of London called Capital Growth that encouraged urban allotments. We applied for the funding, and the City of London agreed to let us clear a site on the estate, on the proviso that it was temporary, and it could be cleared at any time. We set it up with just 20 large bags of soil, and it really took off. It was very exciting — we call ourselves the Golden Lane Baggers, and it's still going and is bigger than ever. There are probably 100 or so people now.

'We came up with the great idea of a market day.'

SO That's amazing, a lot of these types of initiatives don't always last once the novelty runs out.

BB That's what I really like about it, the fact it's sustained itself. It's also a great sun trap, it gets the late sun, and it's a wonderful place just to sit. The allotments are fantastic because they draw everybody in: tenants, leaseholders, young, old, families. A couple of years ago we also tried to rewild the estate, so we have a wildflower meadow, and outside the allotments we planted the pits of the trees with herbs and that sort of thing.

'The allotments are fantastic because they draw everybody in.'

SO Do the residents look after the rest of the green spaces on the estate?

BB No, that's all managed by the City of London, but I think the communal spaces are something we need to have a public consultation on. We are beginning to have discussions about what the impact of the Crossrail, the new railway line, is going to have on Golden Lane. There are a lot of pedestrian routes through the estate, even though it's meant to be a private estate, people come and congregate and have their lunch here. In summer, outside Bayer and Hatfield, it can be packed with people who work nearby having picnics. At the moment it's not really a problem, but with new Crossrail stations at Moorgate and Farringdon, it will dramatically increase footfall. So I think we need to really think about what's public and what's private.

SO The estate attracts a lot of creative people, doesn't it?

BB Absolutely. There are so many young architects, design professionals, curators, artists and photographers that choose to live here. When I first moved here, they were the kind of 'new people' moving in. And that was great because there was a good mix of them and the original keyworkers. But that's changing, it's becoming too extreme. To buy a property here now requires a serious amount of money, and social housing is impossible to get unless it's a critical case or for very vulnerable people. The thing I love about the estate is that there are social tenants who have been here for decades and raised families. It's a real community of people who are emotionally attached to the place. People love being here, and I think that's what unifies it.

SO Can you imagine moving out of Golden Lane?

BB I feel incredibly lucky and privileged to have the opportunity to live here. If I had to move, I'd probably be one of those annoying people that rent it out. I would find it hard to let go of it. Ideally, what I would like to do — if I knew it would be properly managed and looked after — is to put my flat back into social housing. I feel like we are just custodians of it. I have had the pleasure of experiencing it and living here, and I want to give somebody else that same chance. It galls me to see how much these properties cost now, and I think that is really unfair. It's not just a place to live, it's a place you belong to and are a part of.

Howard Sullivan

SO   How did you end up living on Golden Lane Estate?

HS   It's an interesting story. In the summer when I was 20, I did work experience for the Science Museum with one of my university tutors. Our job was to drive around London, picking up and dropping off various things. On one of our missions, we were driving around Clerkenwell and my tutor, who lived in Camden, said, 'I want to take you past this place that I would absolutely love to live in. It's my dream home.' We drove along the Golden Lane side of the estate, and I remember saying, 'Yes, it's great', but actually thinking, 'Oh my God, no way!' I was living in Brighton at the time, and my only experience of London was coming up to go shopping in Oxford Street at weekends. I loved the idea of living in London, but I imagined living in Knightsbridge or Soho. I was clueless!

      About ten years later, after graduating from the Royal College of London, some friends found a flat together. They described it as not looking like much from the outside but very interesting on the inside. I went to their housewarming, and it happened to be a maisonette on Golden Lane Estate. I thought it was just amazing. I eventually ended up moving in and lived there for ages, and I have never really left the estate since.

SO   So you've lived in a few different blocks on the estate?

HS   Yes, I was in Basterfield House first. At that time, some other friends were living in the tower, Great Arthur House, near the top. When I visited them, I thought their flat was incredible, and when they moved out, I ended up renting it for a few years until I got a job working in Australia. When I was out there, I saw, online, that a top floor flat — with the barrel-vaulted ceiling — in Crescent House had come onto the market. A friend of mine who lived on the block offered to go and see it for me, and he was so excited about it. He said it had all the original features, but they had been covered up. The kitchen surfaces had plastic laminate on top, for example, but the original wooden worktop was underneath. I ended up putting an offer in without ever seeing the flat.

SO   That shows how much faith you had in the design of it.

HS   Absolutely, and I had seen my friend's flat, so I knew what they were like, although they are all slightly different combinations. The block is curved and follows the shape of the road; there are variations in what juts out over the street, the window configuration, where the bathroom and kitchen are. And how they are all linked together. When I moved in, I spent six months stripping it all back to the original features. As a designer with years of expertise in detailed architectural drawings, it was a great experience in understanding how much care and attention had been put into the design and the detailing. The window frames, for example, have these beautiful shadow gaps and junctions —they are a work of art. You would never find that level of craftsmanship in a flat built today.

SO   Have you come across other social housing schemes from this period that have a similar level of detailing?

HS   No, never. I'm not an expert in social housing but I have been into quite a few. The Trellick and the Balfron Tower by Ernő Goldfinger, for example, are interesting but the attention to detail is in their communal areas. The lift lobbies, for instance, have beautiful, colourful glass bricks. The experience was intended to uplift you and give you a sense of *joie de vivre*. Most people think of post-war social housing as low-grade and poor quality, but I would beg to differ. I think low-grade housing is what we are seeing in contemporary private residential developments, which are very 'vanilla'. They have low ceilings, zero detailing, poor partitioning and acoustics. They're designed like a sausage machine churning out 'vanilla living', which is not going to inspire anyone. Here on Golden Lane, even the functional features are beautiful and thought through. Every problem has been flipped and turned into an opportunity. There are a lot of elements that set these flats apart. The windows in my flat, for example, rotate, so that you can get a tremendous amount of airflow. In the maisonettes, the double-height glass door, that opens onto the balcony, lifts all the way up. No one would engineer a solution like that now. It was very innovative at the time, and I expect it set a lot of precedents for housing developments.

SO   It's extraordinary that this was their first project, and they didn't have much previous experience.

HS   Is that the case? I didn't realize. That makes complete sense because I think when you're young and emerging, you have so much energy, everything is possible. That really comes across, the design is so fresh, and there is so much energy. I think they tested a lot of ideas: the barrel-vaulted ceilings, the glass curtain walling on high-rise blocks, the cantilevered stairs in low-rise maisonettes, the pond and communal facilities, such as the gym and the tennis courts.

SO   What is it like living here?

HS   It's a phenomenal place to live. I'm the envy of loads of people in my office when I talk about basic things, like the fact I know my neighbours. I could literally borrow a cup of sugar off anyone here. I had a lovely neighbour downstairs, Matt Fretton, who is sadly not with us anymore. He was the son of the architect Tony Fretton. I got to know him quite well through the swimming pool, and it turned out he lived directly underneath me. We used to have coffees and catch up, and he told me his dad explained the principles of the design of the flats in Crescent House. He explained how the diagonal line was crucial in making them feel as spacious as possible. From the kitchen, you have a view all the way through to the living room and through to the street. That's one of the reasons the partitions in the kitchens have glass: not only does the glass make it more sociable as you see people in the living space, but you also have a greater sense of space even though the kitchen is absolutely tiny.

In terms of community, the architects understood that a group of four dwellings is the optimum number for people to make relationships. The minute it gets to six, it gets more complicated. You might like one neighbour but not another for example, so here the courtyards are designed so that the front doors are in batches of four. Consequently, you get to know your little cluster of neighbours. They also designed it so that open walkways have space for plants, and the maisonettes have balconies or communal gardens, to create an opportunity for people to stop and chat. It's very different to the Barbican where the corridors are internal and purely functional, so people tend to walk down them with their heads down. On Golden Lane, everyone is very friendly. The joy of this estate is the fact it's a whole microcosm — housing, a gym, shops and the community centre.

'On Golden Lane, everyone is very friendly. The joy of this estate is the fact it's a whole microcosm — housing, a gym, shops and the community centre.'

SO   With regards to your flat in Crescent House: it's a studio with a separate enclosure for the bed. I think it's just under 40 square metres; with two of you living here, is it big enough?

HS   We are both big hoarders, and I think for two people, it's pushing it. It's a great space, I can't grumble, but although wardrobe space in today's world is a challenge, we have

'The storage in the flat has been designed for a simple way of life.'

made it work. Antonio, my partner, has lots of brilliant hidden storage everywhere. We also have a storage unit outside the flat, which has ended up being more of a messy walk-in wardrobe. We have had to be more thoughtful, for example, by putting all our winter clothes away in the summer. We also read the Marie Kondo book about minimizing all of your possessions. We got rid of a lot of things and lived very minimally for a while, but eventually, life catches up. The book did teach me that the storage in the flat has been designed for a simple way of life: there's a sock drawer, an underwear drawer, drawers for bedding and linen, and there is lots of hanging space. There is enough space for what you need. But we are a generation where we have too much stuff.

SO   Yes exactly, it was designed for people just after the war that wouldn't have had the money for an excessive amount of 'stuff'. So apart from the additional wardrobe, is there anything else you would change about the flat?

HS   I'd love to have a balcony. We have, actually, changed the bedroom area from the original design by adding 'a lid' to the top of the sleeping area. After living in it for a few months in the summer, I realized that while I love the light that comes through the large windows, it was not great at 3 am! But now the bedroom is perfect. It's tiny, but it would feel weird to have a bedroom any bigger. I have got used to it being a place just to go to sleep and not have any clutter. The flat has been designed a bit like a yacht or a boat interior, where everything has a purpose. There are thoughtful details that maximize the space, such as sliding doors.

SO   The compact kitchens, in particular, are very boat-like.

HS   Yes, there's a lot of wood, so they feel like a ship's cabin. We restored the L-shaped hardwood worktop, and what's fantastic is that you could do that again and again to bring it back to its former glory. The sink is stainless steel, and very durable. Its surface doesn't look much different to a new sink even though it's 60 years old. Everything was built to last, using good-quality materials.

SO   Have you ever been tempted to replace it with a modern fitted kitchen?

HS   Never! It works as it is. There's space for a free-standing cooker and a slim fridge, and there are built-in drawers. Everything else is open shelving. I like the idea of keeping it as open as possible, even though that means you do see a lot of crockery, and so on, but when you look into the kitchen, your view is beyond it and is not stopped by a boxy built-in cupboard.

so   Are there any downsides to living on the estate?

HS   For all the fantastic things about the estate, we are actually moving soon. The main reason is we want a garden. We've been talking about getting a dog, and that's not possible here. It's the biggest drawback of living here. I feel very sentimental towards my flat, though. When I first moved here, I remember thinking it would be such a great place to have in old age— to live in the centre of the city and to be able to pop along to the Barbican Centre. My mum helped me decorate it, and soon after we lost her to cancer, so I have a lot of emotion and memories tied up in it. I can't imagine ever selling it.

so   What would you miss most?

HS   The swimming pool. It's the most sociable swimming pool I've ever known. I know at least 20 people. Every day we talk in the changing room, and there's such a variety of characters. There's David who's in his late 80s, who has had two hip replacements but still swims two or three times a week. There are City people who come and go, and then you never see them again. There's Martin who fixes watches and is in his 50s—he has a quick swim and then goes home. For a lot of people, it's an essential part of their social life. We chit-chat about everything, and nothing is off-limits.

David Ish-Horowicz
and Rosamund Diamond

SO   When did you move to Golden Lane Estate?

DIH   We've been here since about 2000. The laboratory where I work had moved down to London from Oxford in 1995. We procrastinated for a few years before realizing we had to buy something, as although prices were relatively low, they were beginning to creep up.

SO   Did you already know about the estate?

DIH   Ros, who is an architect, did. She talked about it quite often, but I didn't know anything about it.

RD   David's lab was in Lincoln's Inn Fields, and I remember he said to me, 'I want to be 20-minute walk from the lab'. I laughed and said, 'Well I think it's going to have to be social housing of some sort because we won't be able to afford anything else'. Golden Lane Estate was under the radar back then—it was significantly undervalued compared to places around it. I'd lost interest in trying to find us a flat, but one day one of the estate agents called me and said something like, 'A flat in a place called Golden Lane Estate has come up —I don't really know where it is, but would you be interested in seeing it?'

SO   Why was it so undervalued?

DIH   It had the stigma of being social housing. Ros phoned me up to tell me we were going to see this flat, and I knew we would end up living here because she had talked so much about the estate.

SO   Do you know who had lived in the flat before you?

RD   The people we bought from had bought it under the Right to Buy scheme. It was a double family—they had two young kids from their own marriage, and two older kids from previous marriages. The husband was a policeman, and so fitted perfectly with the original profile for this estate. They sold the flat and moved to the coast into a new-build house, which could accommodate the whole of the family. What we like about our flat, which is in Stanley Cohen House, is the east/west light. The other thing I've begun to realize is that the culture of Stanley Cohen House is a bit different from the other blocks, there's a different dynamic. When we moved in, there were a lot of older people around us, including the vestiges of the old Jewish community. There's a good mix of people here, and we all get along very well.

SO I suppose you have a lot more communal space in Stanley Cohen House, so is there more opportunity to interact with neighbours than some of the other blocks?

DIH Yes, although we didn't know any of this before moving in. It looked nice, fitted the bill, and we could just about afford it.

SO There are now several new housing developments in the area, but in the late 1990s, apart from the Barbican, there wasn't much else.

DIH That's right, but within five years of us moving here, that changed.

RD At the time I remember if I had a problem with my bike, for example, I would have to go all the way to Gray's Inn Road, a 20-minute walk, which was a real pain. Now we have a trendy bike shop at the end of the road, and so many other things like that.

SO But did it still feel central?

RD Yes, especially as we cycle everywhere. The design brigade, the architects etc., were moving their studios in this direction. When I was looking for an office 15 years ago, I looked at a building across the way, but it was a bit too expensive. I suggested to a colleague to look north of Old Street, in Shoreditch, as it was a lot cheaper. But that area has gradually caught up and become gentrified. Step by step, people have been forced to move further and further east, where the prices are lower.

DIH Having a bicycle in central London changes the way you think about it. I can cycle from home to Tottenham Court Road in 15 minutes.

SO And what about the estate itself; how has that changed over the years?

DIH I think one of the things that has changed is that the estate office feels much less integrated than it did. Generally, the Corporation does not see its role as facilitating; it concentrates more on controlling and spending as little money as possible. The estate office staff used to live on the estate, and they identified themselves with the residents. Now it's just a job. When we first moved here, they did quite a lot for us, such as taking in parcels.

SO   What about the community; how has that changed?

RD   Some residents have a very strong communal commitment. The estate allotments, for example, are fantastic, and it has a great mix of tenants and leaseholders.

SO   Are you involved in the residents' association?

RD   We're active in some areas that affect the estate—but it's very time-consuming and complicated. The council are planning to replace the windows across the estate and have appointed the architects Studio Partington, who were also responsible for refurbishing the community centre. Bringing modernist architecture up to contemporary standards, in terms of heat loss, is almost more challenging than for Edwardian or Victorian architecture because the window sections are so small. Upgrading to double glazing is very noticeable, and it changes the overall character of the fenestration. When I looked at the detailing of the recent replacement of the Great Arthur House windows, I thought, given the limitations, they didn't do a bad job. The way the project was delivered, however, was a different matter. My architecture practice worked on a flat in Basterfield House, and we added secondary glazing. We were meticulous. But replacing all the windows is going to be very complicated. When the estate was built, different builders did different buildings, and nothing was standardized. There was a terrible shortage of materials due to it being just after the war, building standards were not great, and the combination of all of those things is going to make it extremely challenging.

SO   Have you added double glazing to your own flat?

RD   When we first moved in, we did an inexpensive, limited, budget renovation. Ten years later, I did it more seriously with an excellent team of Polish builders. They rubbed all the window frames down and found holes that ran straight through the frames. I had to do something about it very quickly, and I got permission from the Conservation Department to replace the windows with double glazing.

The flats don't have any insulation, and if the plan is to replace all the windows across the estate, it makes sense also to insulate the underneath of them. But I think the City of London will do the minimum it needs to. Despite it being a wealthy borough, the council claim they don't have a lot of money for maintaining its social housing stock.

SO   As it's a Grade II-listed estate, you would think they would have a pot of money outside of the normal housing budget. You can't compare it to an estate where it doesn't need the same level of work to meet listed building standards.

RD   Indeed, and if they are trying to bring the housing up to a better standard, they have to do it properly. You have to do everything you can when you have scaffolding up. The council has an advantage nowadays because 50 per cent of the estate is in private ownership; they don't have to pay 100 per ocnt of the cost.

DIH   I think the City perceives cost-saving, rather than good quality or value for money, as its main priority. But all these things withstanding, we are still very happy to live here!

RD   Yes, we love it!

SO   For all the gripes, it seems everybody that lives here or even people that visit, have a real warmth towards the place.

RD   Yes, our neighbours across the way used to live in the Barbican Estate until recently, and they much prefer the fact Golden Lane Estate is very personable. It has a good mix of private and social tenants.

DIH   I have noticed, recently, generations of kids growing up together and mixing. I think that's great and is increasingly rare. Nearby we have the new posh Denizen apartments on Golden Lane, which will have a cinema in the basement and all sorts of luxury facilities. Then there's a social housing tower being squeezed into the former site of Richard Cloudesley School, next to Basterfield House. It's two extremes.

SO   What do you think makes Golden Lane a successful estate?

RD   There is a good mix of sizes of flats, which means you get a mixture of people living here—families, single people, old and young people, and that's how it should be. The openness and the configuration of the estate also mean you get the public walking through it. One of the fundamental issues with

'The openness and the configuration of the estate also mean you get the public walking through it.'

post-war medium- to low-rise housing estates in London is that they were designed based on the idea of defensible space, which segregated ordinary movement from estates. That's one of the main reasons they developed social problems. Natural surveillance, such as in Golden Lane Estate, is the best way of preventing anti-social behaviour. The constant mix and flow of people works extremely well. I think Golden Lane is a model for how to do housing.

Lucy Johnston

so   How long have you lived on Golden Lane Estate?

LJ   My family moved here in 1993 when I was 12. We were living in
another Corporation of London housing estate, Windsor house
on Wenlock Road, in a little three-bed maisonette. When the
council discovered asbestos in the walls, they either rehoused
people in another block or to another Corporation of London
estate. Although there were four of us — my parents, me and
my sister — they offered us a two-bedroom maisonette in
Bowater House. My sister was about to go to university, and
they promised her a studio flat in Crescent House for when
she returned. I don't think that would happen now.

so   Did your parents grow up in London?

LJ   I'm from a very working-class family. My dad is originally from
Ireland; my mum is from the East End. Living in social housing
was fantastic as it gave me and my sister, Ella, the opportunity
to go to university and have access to some of the things my
parents didn't.

so   Were your parents familiar with Golden Lane Estate before
they moved here?

LJ   Absolutely. It was considered the jewel in the crown of the
Corporation of London housing estates. I remember seeing
Great Arthur House tower from our old flat, and I always
thought it was an incredible modernist structure with what
looked like an aeroplane on top of it. We knew the area quite
well already — I used to go to Whitecross Street with my nan,
where there used to be a market every Saturday. My parents
would take me to the Barbican Centre, to free live music
events, which was brilliant. So when we moved to Golden
Lane, it was a dream come true.

so   What was the estate like when you moved here? And how
did it compare to where you had been living?

LJ   Windsor House was very different — a large, red-brick
Victorian estate, but it had a real sense of community.

> 'My parents
> thought if we
> moved to
> Golden Lane, it
> would be a safer
> place for me
> and my sister.'

My dad had lived there since he was 16, and my mum lived two minutes up the road. It was a little bit rough, and my parents thought if we moved to Golden Lane, it would be a safer place for me and my sister, with fewer robberies and muggings. When we first moved here, the estate was impeccable — it was very well looked after. There were helpful people in the estate office, the exterior of the blocks was painted every so often, that sort of thing.

SO Do you remember what you thought of the flat when you first moved there?

LJ I remember feeling a lot more at ease. It sounds silly, but in my last place, it felt haunted. It was a beautiful flat, but the upstairs had weird energy. On Golden Lane, the design of the maisonette was much more open, we had a balcony too, and overall, it made me feel happier.

SO Did you know anybody who already lived on the estate?

LJ No, not at all, but we got to know our neighbours. We had a lovely lady next door called Jean. Sadly, a lot of the people that have been my neighbours have since passed away. In the flat that I am in now, in Crescent House, I had a wonderful neighbour called Nancy, who lived until she was 101 years old, and she'd been on the estate for years. I loved going into her flat as it had a lot of the original features. Then there was Bert, across the way, who was also one of the original residents, but he has just recently died. I think it's quite unusual for somebody my age to have lived here for so long. It's quite sad seeing so many of the original residents pass away.

SO What was it like being a teenager on the estate?

LJ It felt like I was one of the only teenagers here. There was a year, at around the age of 14 or 15, where I just didn't want to go to school, and the best place to play truant was the Barbican because you would never bump into anyone. I would go to the chip shop on Whitecross Street and then go to the Barbican, sometimes with a mate, and read or listen to music, or wander around the conservatory. It was, and still is, my sanctuary. I remember when my mum found out I had been skipping school, she took me to see *Romeo and Juliet* at the theatre in the Barbican Centre. I managed to get top marks in my exam! Even though I didn't have loads of teenage friends in the area, having access to the culture, which was free, especially as a working-class kid, was life-changing.

SO   By the time you moved here in the 1990s, had a lot of the flats already sold through the Right to Buy scheme?

LJ   Yes, and my parents eventually also bought their council flat, which they were able to buy on a relatively low income and at a reasonable rate. That wouldn't be the case now. They have since sold their flat and moved out of London.

SO   How has the estate changed over the years?

LJ   It's not as well cared for now as it was when my parents were here. Back then, it felt like the Corporation protected and respected the estate. Some years ago, there was an incident where the council decided to charge for the external storage units that come with the flats. They didn't have proper records of who had what, and to cut a long story short, they ended up throwing away everything I had in my storage unit. It was devastating. The estate office was dismissive and handled the situation badly. That's when I first noticed a shift in management. As someone who loves Golden Lane, I feel protective of it, and I want it to be looked after properly, however the constant battle with the Corporation is challenging. Luckily the community here is still very strong, and if I were ever to leave it, I would really miss it. The Barbican Estate is great, but Golden Lane is like its weird little sister, even though it's older. It's like the person you want to sit next to at a dinner party because they have some really fascinating stories.

'The flats are flooded with natural light, and are a joy to photograph.'

SO   What do you like about the architecture?

LJ   It is very open, even though it's a private estate. You are spoilt for light living here. The flats are flooded with natural light, and are a joy to photograph. The living room in our Bowater House maisonette had huge double-height windows. My parents hated the fact that there was no overhead lighting, but you didn't need it. After Bowater, I moved into a studio in Cullum Welch House. It had one long room with the original parquet floor at one end and quarry tiles at the other, and full-width windows. It was beautiful. I love walking by the pond or the tennis courts. It still feels like a place where you can get a breather from the city, it's a little oasis.

SO   Were you aware of the design, and its uniqueness, when you moved here?

LJ   Very much so, especially coming from a Victorian flat which felt and looked very different. My parents were funny — they had never lived in a modernist flat before and had a temptation to fight the aesthetic and to make it look homely. I remember when we moved here, my dad put wooden radiator boxes on all the radiators. Eventually, they realized you just have to go with the design — you can't fight it. And once you embrace it, the flats are beautiful as they are. In Crescent House, where I live now, most of my furniture is mid-century because it fits and is the right proportion; you can't try and make it look like a traditional house.

SO It sounds as if living here has shaped your taste?

LJ I think so. Especially coming from a working-class background, being given a flat to live in that you would only see in magazines was amazing. In the maisonette, the stairs jut out of the wall as if they are floating. Friends would come over and would say, 'Wow, you've got *Flight of the Navigator* stairs!' It felt very special. The creative atmosphere on the estate, and the way the flats feel so open, light and unique — compared to anywhere else I saw growing up — sparked a creative curiosity in me. It was that exposure that led me to pursue those passions as I got older. The estate's colourful facades and perfectly designed geometric blocks were a constant source of inspiration when learning photography at the age of 18. I used to take endless photos of the blocks and the spaces in between. I never stopped really. It's not just the architecture that inspired me, but the little sparks of personality that you see throughout the estate: on the balconies, through the windows or in the planters along the walkways.

Someone came to visit me recently, and as they walked up the stairs in Crescent House they were amazed, and said it felt like being on holiday. And it does. In the summer there are people sat outside having coffee and a chat. It's always felt comforting to know behind everyone's front door there are other weird and wonderful souls.

SO So you were proud to live here when you were younger, but was there any stigma because you were a council tenant?

LJ No, not at all. I think when you're a council tenant, you tend to know and mix with other people that live in council flats. I didn't know people who lived in houses. It wasn't until I was older that I realized not everyone lived in a flat. I had a sense of pride in living here. It's unique, and it never felt like social housing was a negative thing. It wasn't until I went to university that I realized some people viewed council housing very differently. I found myself trying to educate people into understanding that private landlords aren't, and shouldn't, always be the norm. I remember speaking to someone who

'Being given a flat to live in that you would only see in magazines was amazing.'

thought that everyone who lived in council housing was getting some kind of benefit. He insisted that it was discounted — but it's not, it's just reasonably priced housing. By paying social rent, you are paying back into the system, as opposed to paying private landlords for them to make a profit. This estate was built for people who lived and worked in the City. My parents didn't earn a lot of money, and I wouldn't have got to where I am today had it not been for secure and safe housing.

In conversation   Lisa Scott and Paul Drinkwater

SO You have fairly recently moved to the estate: what made you want to live on Golden Lane?

PD Lisa and I were living separately: she was in Walthamstow, and I was in Southgate in north London. Three years ago, we decided to buy a place together. I'm a bit of a geek when it comes to modernist architecture, and we both wanted something interesting but were less fussy about the location. I had been on a walking tour of the estate many years ago, so Golden Lane was on our radar. It took us a while to sell our flats because it was just after the Brexit referendum, and one Sunday night we stumbled across the estate agent's listing for the flat we are in now.

LS We knew that the maisonettes hardly ever came up for sale. We saw it on a Monday and decided to put in an offer that very same evening. It got accepted the next day.

PD It was a big lifestyle change for both of us. I grew up in the Home Counties and lived in the suburbs, and our previous flats were quite big, so it was a bit of a moment of madness when we decided to buy a place that is a lot smaller. We sold our car and half of our possessions.

SO Why were you so keen to live in a modernist building?

PD I'd always lived in functional flats. My previous home was an early 1990s building, and it wasn't an exciting place to live. I used to work at RIBA (Royal Institute of British Architects), as the director of data and technology, and I think that fired up my interest in architecture. My first memories of modernist architecture were growing up in Woking, Surrey, where there is a big, Brutalist tower that belongs to British American Tobacco. When I was small, I used to look at what seemed like a huge skyscraper, in awe. That's where the seed was sown. I have a theory that the things you remember as a child, whether it be music or architecture, you become slightly obsessed with in later life. The dream would have been to live in the Barbican, but that was beyond what we could afford — Golden Lane seemed like the next best thing.

SO So the attraction is partly nostalgia?

PD Partly. I had an aunt and uncle who lived in the suburbs of Oxford in what we called the upside-down house, where the bedrooms were on the ground floor and the living space at the top. And that sense of it being different and interesting really made an impression on me.

LS I'd always lived in Victorian conversions. I didn't know anything about modernist architecture. When you meet somebody, I think you inherit and absorb some of their obsessions and the things they like. When we started viewing post-war, architect-designed flats, I was soon on board. I liked their clean lines, the light and the feeling of space. Although I had never lived on an estate, I liked the idea of it, and when I researched Golden Lane, I knew I would love it.

SO What kind of research did you do?

LS Mainly about the history and the architecture. Despite it being right next to the Barbican, it's incredible how little known it is. It's very popular with architects and designers though, and they are very passionate about it. I remember when I told my colleagues I was buying a flat on Golden Lane, the designers there suddenly popped their heads up and wanted to have a look at the pictures of it, and they were drooling at the staircase.

'Despite it being right next to the Barbican, it's incredible how little known it is.'

SO What were your first impressions of the estate?

PD When I came on that walking tour, I remember being struck by the contrast of coming off the busy road and walking into the estate. It was a tranquil oasis, with the calming 'thwock, thwock' sound coming from the tennis court.

LS When I first came to look at the flat, my abiding memory was seeing a Pret A Manger and a Costa coffee shop, and I thought, 'Yes!' In Southgate, it was a 25-minute walk to the shop, so to have cafes on our doorstep is amazing. Old Street is just around the corner, as is Clerkenwell—I used to travel to these places for a night out, and now they are within walking distance.

SO Has living here lived up to your expectations?

PD The location certainly has. And the estate has too. I think what makes it special is the community.

LS Before we moved here, we got involved with the community as much as we could. We put our names down for the allotment. We met Sue Pearson, who lives in our block and is our local councillor. We went to the residents' meetings about the construction site next to us. And we kept seeing the same faces, so it was easy to get involved. There are some people on the estate that are very motivated and community-driven; people have been very friendly and welcoming in that respect. And since I've had a baby, I've met a different group of people.

SO   Had you planned for it to be a family home?

LS   No, it wasn't planned. When I first came to view the flat, there was a baby gate at the bottom of the stairs. I remember thinking, 'God, can you imagine having a baby here?' It didn't seem impossible, but it didn't seem like an obvious choice. We didn't buy it thinking it was our 'forever home'.

PD   We seem to be in the middle of a baby boom on the estate at the moment. After we had our baby, our next-door neighbours had a daughter two days later and then so did a few other people across the estate.

SO   How is the space with a baby?

LS   It's okay. I spend all my time in the lounge, which has essentially become a baby's playroom, so I think we could make better use of the bedrooms. Our daughter is only ten months old, but Paul said the other day that the flat feels a lot smaller with a third person in it.

'We sold a lot of our things before we moved here and bought furniture to fit the proportions of the flat, so it's very liveable.'

PD   We sold a lot of our things before we moved here and bought furniture to fit the proportions of the flat, so it's very liveable. It's never felt tiny —but suddenly when you have a baby and all the stuff that brings, it can be quite challenging — especially being next to a building site. Some days, even when it's hot, we have to keep all the windows shut because of all the grime and noise, and that isn't easy.

SO   You're right next to the new primary school that is currently being built. How much did you know about it before you moved here?

PD   We knew there was a planning application to demolish the Richard Cloudesley School that was on the site, and it would be replaced with something. What we hadn't anticipated, maybe naively, is the sheer scale of it and the council's attempt to cram a big residential block, along with the school, onto the same site. Also, how close it is to our flat.

It's difficult not to have a rant about it, but the whole planning process was a bit of a disgrace.

LS   Our solicitor brought it to our attention and suggested we might consider pulling out. But at the time, I thought there was a reasonable chance it would not get planning permission. So right from the start, we were involved in objecting.

PD   We weren't objecting to a school or social housing on the site, but the appalling design of it. There was such a missed opportunity to take the ethos of Golden Lane Estate and to build on that. I think there's a lack of democracy in the City of London that trickles down, and decisions are made, and pockets lined.

SO   How did the estate, in general, react to the proposal of the school and block of flats?

LS   During the planning phase, there were huge residents' meetings, and there was a lot of activism and protests against it.

PD   But, eventually, people got worn down by it and felt very powerless. The relationship between the City of London and the residents has now broken down. I think the City see the value of the Barbican Estate, maybe because there are a lot of influential people living there, but not so for Golden Lane.

SO   What was your perception of the City of London before you moved here?

LS   I presumed the City held Golden Lane Estate in equal esteem to the Barbican, but soon realized the reality. You can see it in the upkeep of the estate: there's paint peeling off the walls, things are broken, and it's starting to look really shabby. Jobs are outsourced, and often inadequately briefed. So a contractor comes in, does the job badly, and then that needs to be fixed. And it's not cheap to live here — we pay several hundred pounds a quarter in service charges. When we first moved in, they were replacing the lifts, and I remember thinking if these are the new ones, what did the old ones look like! Everything is just a bit shoddy.

SO   I think people feel very sad about the lack of maintenance because they love the estate so much.

PD   Yes, it's just terrible management; there's no other way of putting it. It's a shame because the estate could be fantastic.

'Suddenly in
the heart of the
city, we were
in the middle
of a carnival,
it was amazing.'

The refurbishment of Great Arthur House has been great, and to see it returned to its former glory gives you a hint of what the whole estate could look like with a little bit of will. I hope somebody in the City of London will recognize the value of the estate, appreciate it and see through the improvements it needs. It's a beautiful estate. There are times on a sunny day when you can see the sunset gleaming off the swimming pool, and my soul lifts. Last year during a garden open day, I was on the balcony, and there was a brass band playing outside and the Red Arrows flying overhead. Suddenly in the heart of the city, we were in the middle of a carnival, it was amazing. But because it can be so wonderful, it makes it even more frustrating to see the wheels falling off.

Michelle Praag

SO How long have you lived on Golden Lane Estate?

MP I've been here since I was 18 months old. When I was born, my mum and dad were living with my grandmother in Windsor House off City Road, another City of London estate. My grandmother managed to get a new flat on Golden Lane Estate, and we all moved into Cuthbert Harrowing House, the first block completed, in 1956. We lived there for a while, but it was only a two-bedroom flat, so when I was 12, my parents managed to get their own maisonette, at the top of Bowater House. My mum still lives there, and I live on the ground floor of the same block.

SO So you have lived on the estate your whole life?

MP Almost. When I got married, my husband and I moved to Barkingside, but I didn't like it, and I wanted to move back. I missed the community of the estate and the fact that everything is so nearby. I missed the people and the hustle and bustle. We stayed in Barkingside for about a year, and even though we knew a lot of people there, we decided to come back and move in with my mum. We got ourselves on the housing list and eventually got our own flat, initially in Bayer House, and then managed to transfer to my current flat in Bowater, which has three bedrooms.

SO What was it like growing up here when the estate was brand new?

MP To me, it was just normal. I didn't know anything else, so I suppose I took it for granted. There were a lot of other children on the estate, and it was great playing together. Times were different then, there wasn't much to do, and we would spend our time outdoors playing with a football or climbing things. I remember the porters who worked in the estate office were quite strict. They were always telling us not to do something. The estate was relatively quiet then, and some of the other residents would also tell us off for making too much noise. I remember this one time I was outside with my friends playing and making a lot of noise, and the people who used to live in the flat I'm in now threw a bucket of water over us!

SO   Did you go to any of the organized activities for children?

MP   There were several classes in the community centre, such as a Saturday morning cinema club and ballet, which I hated as I much preferred climbing trees.

SO   Did your mum know people living on the estate when she first moved here?

MP   No, but she soon got to know people, and she made a lot of friends. It was easy to make friends here. Most of the people from my mum's generation have sadly passed away now, and a lot of the people I knew have moved away. It was a very friendly place.

SO   Has that changed?

'It's not full of enormous tower blocks. We have just one high-rise.'

MP   It has changed over the years. More people are renting privately now, but I wouldn't say it was better or worse. As you get older, your priorities change, and things change around you, so you have to learn to go along with it and adapt. Some of the older people might think it's not the same as the 'good old days', but I like change. It's good to be moving forward. I would say there is still a solid community here, which is fantastic. We have a WhatsApp group for our block, so if anyone has any problems or needs a hand with something, we all help each other out, and it's a great way of keeping in touch. A charity is running a food bank in the community centre at the moment, and that's attracted a lot of volunteers. I have a younger cousin who is in her 20s and has recently moved to the estate; she's helping out with the food bank and loves the community here. What's great about this estate is that it attracts all ages.

SO   What do you think it is about this estate that makes it such a friendly place?

MP   I'm not sure. Maybe it's because it's not full of enormous tower blocks. We have just one high-rise. I can be sitting outside on my mobility scooter, having a cigarette, and the amount of people that pass by, say hello or stop for a chat is incredible. It's like a little village.

SO   The area must have changed a lot since you were little?

MP   I remember the Barbican going up very well. I used to be able

'I used to be able
to look out of
my window and
see right across
to St Paul's
Cathedral.'

to look out of my window and see right across to St Paul's Cathedral, which was amazing. There was nothing in front of us but the bomb site, which we would play on when we were kids. When they started building the Barbican, it was very exciting. I remember there were film crews, photographers and that sort of thing.

SO The architecture of the Barbican often divides people. What did you think of the look of the new buildings?

MP I loved it, it looked so impressive. I used to think to myself, 'If only I could afford a place there'.

SO What was the rest of the area like; were there shops and places to go?

MP There was Whitecross Street market, which was much busier than it is now. Now it's just a food market, but back then it sold everything: haberdashery, butchers, green-grocers, baby clothes. The only other shops were the ones under Crescent House, on Goswell Road. I remember there was a jewellery shop, the greengrocers, the hardware store and a little sweet shop at the end. Not too different from what they are now.

SO Today they seem a little underused: were they busier then?

MP Even back then, they were underused. They were quite old-fashioned shops, and people preferred to shop on Whitecross Street, or go up to Islington to Chapel market.

SO It must have been exciting for your parents to move into a brand-new flat: do you know what they thought of it?

MP My mum would be able to tell you some great stories about it, but she's not been well, unfortunately. I remember she furnished the flat with all new furniture. It was all red and grey, including the carpet. It was quite posh at the time. She had a washing machine, a top loader with a big clothes mangle that sat on top. But before that, she used the laundry room next to the estate office, on the ground floor of Great Arthur House. They're planning to turn that space into flats, but at the time it was the laundry room. You had to book a slot, and my mum would go once a week, and sometimes I would go with her. There was also a room next to the laundry for a camera club, with a darkroom. That mainly attracted the men living on the estate.

SO Have you brought up your own family here?

MP Yes, I have a son and a daughter. My son lives in Weymouth, and my daughter lives in Sidcup, but she spends a lot of time with me and still has a bedroom here. Her work is nearby, and she loves it here. It was great being a mum here and being part of the estate. All the mums would meet up in the park, and the kids would play together; it was very nice.

SO Did they enjoy growing up here?

MP Yes, they both went to the Italia Conti School, which is just across the road. It's a performing arts school. They were both into dancing, so it was great to have the school on our doorstep. I think growing up here has made them confident and independent. But they couldn't afford to stay living in central London now. It's so expensive.

SO Were you ever tempted to buy your flat from the council?

MP No, but my mum bought hers. So she is a leaseholder, and I'm not sure she's better off. The service charges are so high that I am glad I didn't buy mine. If something goes wrong in my flat and I need a repair, yes, I pay for it through the rent, but it's a more straightforward process to get it repaired and not so much of a worry. And there are a lot of things wrong with these flats now. Not in the design, but they are 60 years old, and things are going wrong. They are talking about replacing the windows, but I'm not sure if they ever will. As I live on the corner, in the winter, it's freezing, and I end up spending a lot of money on energy bills.

SO Do you ever imagine moving out of the estate?

MP Sometimes, when I feel fed up with London. It feels too dirty and busy. During the week it's jam-packed with people who work in the area, and I sometimes think wouldn't it be nice to live in the country. That's when I consider moving out. But in reality, I don't think I could put up with it for more than a couple of weeks. I'd miss Golden Lane too much. Whenever I am away from London, and I come back and cross one of the bridges over the Thames, I think, 'Yes! Home.'

This page and opposite   Views into the living space of a one-room flat in Stanley
Cohen House (see plan on page 155). The long, horizontal
block—in contrast with the taller blocks on the scheme
—runs along the west side of Golden Lane, and acts as a
barrier between the enclosed courts of the estate and
the road.

The kitchen of a one-room flat in Stanley Cohen House.
The flat faces east, towards Golden Lane.

This page

The colonnaded pavement of Stanley Cohen House, facing Golden Lane, with Great Arthur House in the background. The brick infill is a later addition.

Following page

View across Basterfield lawn and towards the west elevation of Stanley Cohen House. On the ground floor are one-room flats, and on the top floor are one-bedroom flats with large balconies.

View towards the east-facing balcony of a two-bedroom
flat in Stanley Cohen House (see page 156 for plan).

View from the living space towards the kitchen hatch
in a two-bedroom flat in Stanley Cohen House.

Views of one of the bedrooms in Stanley Cohen House, looking west towards the swimming pool and Crescent House; and across the communal Basterfield lawn.

Great Arthur House, the 16-storey tower at the heart of the estate. The defining feature of the tower and the maisonette blocks is the bright yellow, bright red or blue opaque glass cladding set under the windows. This continuity brings coherence to the estate, despite the diversity of the buildings.

A typical flat in Great Arthur House. The building contains 120 one-bedroom flats (see page 157 for plan). To save space, the bedrooms are entered through the living room, with a large sliding partition dividing the two zones. Each flat has a generous balcony with a built-in concrete planter.

View of the kitchen hatch in a Great Arthur House flat.

View towards the balcony of a Great Arthur House flat.

Letter box detail, Great Arthur House.

Bright yellow bin chutes are located on every other floor at both the north and south ends of the block of Great Arthur House.

Previous pages   Exterior views of Crescent House.

Views of a typical one-room flat in Crescent House (see page 158 for plan). The compact apartments are carefully and economically planned. To allow maximum light into the interiors, a three-quarter-height wall with integral up-lighters separates the living room and sleeping area, and a part-glazed partition with built-in shelving and a serving hatch separates the kitchen and the dining area.

Grade II* Crescent House was an extension to the original scheme, intended to incorporate housing for 400 people without losing the character of the overall design. The long horizontal block, facing Goswell Road, echoes Stanley Cohen House on the east side of the estate. Raised on pilotis, the building stands at 4-storeys high, with flats on either side of a central corridor. At the south end of the block (pictured), access is around open courts.

View of a top floor flat in Crescent House, which has distinctive barrel-vaulted ceilings.

Detail of an original kitchen with hardwood work surface
and splash-back and a circular stainless steel sink.

View across the vaulted roofs of Crescent House.

View towards the rear of Cullum Welch House, showing the access gallery. Crescent House is on the right with the parade of shops beneath.

A letter box at Cullum Welch House. The 6-storey block contains 72, south-facing, one-room flats and formed part of the 1954 extension of the estate. Flats are reached via access galleries on each floor. The window frames and doors are painted in tomato red, to echo the primary colours in the earlier blocks.

A kitchen (partly modernized) in Cullum Welch House
(see page 157 for plan).

This page, top

Living space of a studio flat in Cullum Welch House, the smallest unit of all the flats. To delineate the sleeping zone from the living space, half of the floor is covered in quarry tiles, the other in finger parquet.

Bottom

Tenants' stores under Cullum Welch House, leading to the tennis courts.

Detail of a concrete planter, with holes for flower pots, in Cullum Welch House. Beyond are the drum light-wells over the underground car park (see following page) in the main pedestrian piazza.

Previous pages   Views of the physical recreational spaces: the swimming pool, squash court, tennis court (originally planned as a bowling green) and the single-storey club rooms beyond.

This page, top   One of the entrances to Stanley Cohen House.

     Bottom   Ground floor of Basterfield House.

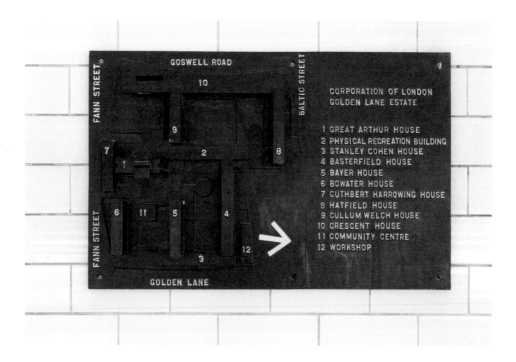

This page, top — The lift lobby in Crescent House, which also serves Cullum Welch House.

Bottom — A three-dimensional cast aluminium estate map. The signage across the estate was produced by Robert W Coan Ltd, an aluminium foundry based in Clerkenwell.

Views of Hatfield House, which formed part of the phase two extension. The block has three levels of 2-storey maisonettes, and a single storey of one-room flats — with south-facing gardens — on the lower ground floor.

A one-room garden flat in Hatfield House (see page 154 for plan). As in Cullum Welch House, the floor is divided in two with quarry tiles and finger parquet. Space for a single bed was placed in a recess, next to the kitchen. Both can be completely concealed behind a sliding timber partition.

View from Fann Street towards Bowater House. The block was one of the first on the estate to be completed. It comprises 30 2-storey maisonettes. Access galleries are on every other floor. The concrete balconies were initially left raw, but weathered quickly and were subsequently painted white.

Staircase to Bowater House.

A living room of a top floor two-bedroom maisonette in Bowater House (see page 152 for plan). The stairs differ from the standard maisonettes on the lower floors; here bookshelves are neatly inserted into the underside of each step.

A top-lit landing of a top floor maisonette.

A south-facing maisonette balcony.

The glass partition between the kitchen and living room
of a top floor maisonette.

Previous page

This page

View towards Bayer House and the low level court with decorative geometric paving, and a pond with playful stepping stones. The community centre is on the left.

A typical two-bedroom maisonette (see page 151 for plan), with cantilevered concrete stairs and partly glazed screen and hatch between the kitchen and dining space.

The living room of a ground floor maisonette in Bayer House, with views towards the balcony and communal gardens beyond. The double-height window features a vertically sliding balcony door.

An original kitchen in a typical maisonette, with a north-facing window. All kitchens, and bathrooms, in the maisonettes have natural light and ventilation.

One of the bedrooms in a two-bedroom maisonette.

View of Bayer House balconies and gardens.

Maisonette blocks

● Typical two-bedroom maisonette

● Three-bedroom maisonette, with
third bedroom on the lower floor

Maisonette blocks

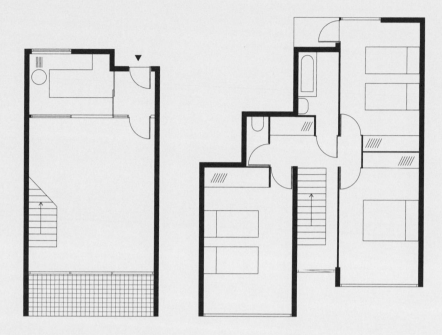

● Three-bedroom maisonette,
with all bedrooms on the upper floor

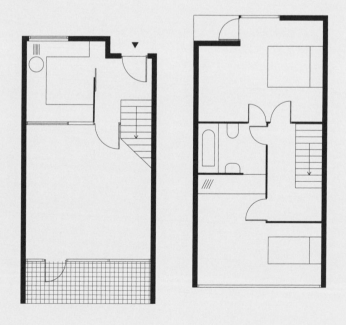

● Top floor two-bedroom maisonette

Maisonette blocks

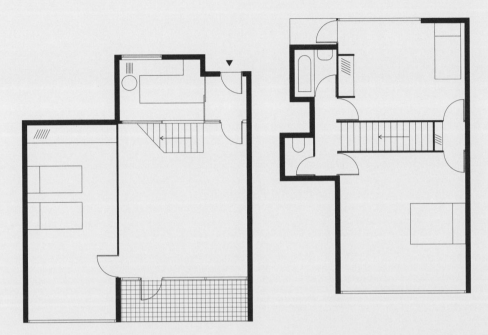

● Top floor three-bedroom maisonette,
with third bedroom on the upper floor

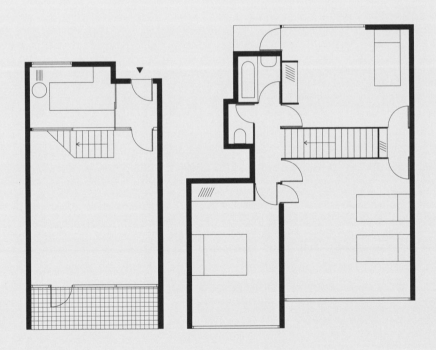

● Top floor three-bedroom maisonette,
with third bedroom on the lower floor

Maisonette blocks

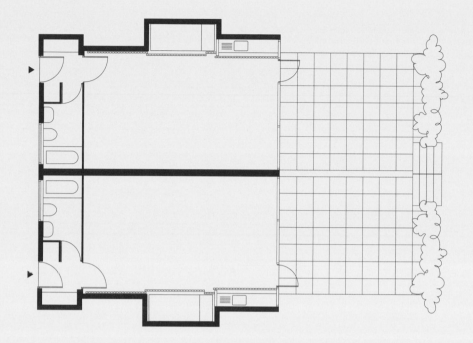

● One-room garden flats in Hatfield House

Stanley Cohen House

154

● Ground floor one-room flat

Stanley Cohen House

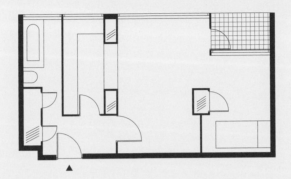

● One-room flat

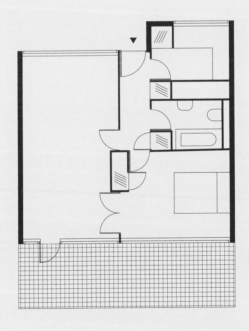

● One-bedroom top floor flat

Stanley Cohen House

● Two-bedroom flat

● Two-bedroom flat

Great Arthur House

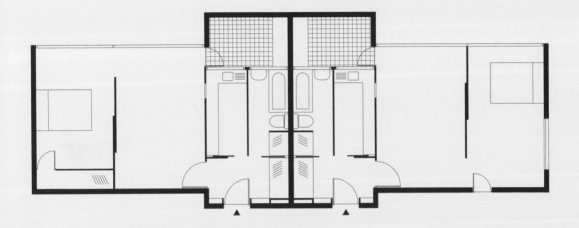

● End and middle of block
one-bedroom flats

Cullum Welch House

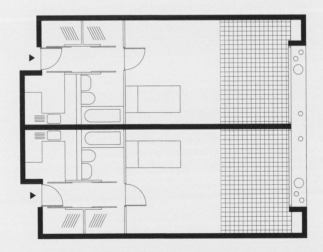

● One-room flats

Crescent House

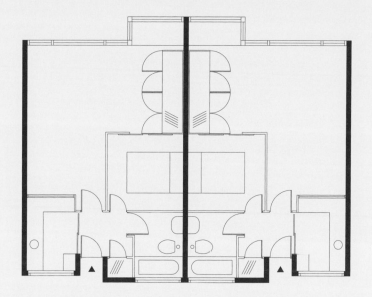

● Typical studio/one-bedroom flats

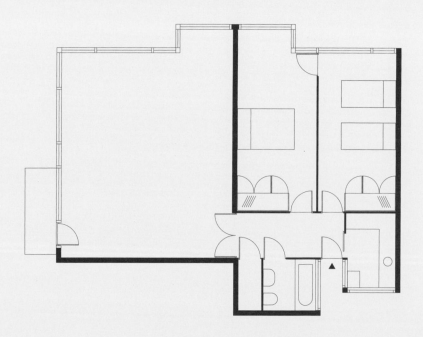

● Two-bedroom corner flat

Further reading

Publications

Modern Flats
F R S Yorke and Frederick Gibberd
Architectural Press, 1958

Modern Architecture in Britain:
Selected examples of recent building
Trevor Dannatt
Batsford, 1959

Chamberlin, Powell and Bon
Elain Harwood
RIBA Publishing, 2011

Estates: An Intimate History
Lynsey Hanley
Granta, 2012

Modernist Estates:
The Buildings and the People who Live
in them Today
Stefi Orazi
Frances Lincoln, 2015

Towers for the Welfare State:
An Architectural History of British
Multi-storey Housing 1945–1970
Stefan Muthesius and Miles Glendinning
University of Edinburgh, 2017

Film

Look at Life: Top People
Special Features Division of the
Rank Organisation
1960

The War Game
Dir. Mai Zettering
1962

The Living City
Produced by the City of London Corporation
1970

Classic Homes Episode One: Tower Blocks
First broadcast on Channel 4 in 1998

The View From My Window Tells Me I'm Home
Esther Johnson
2012

First published in the United Kingdom in 2021 by
B. T. Batsford
43 Great Ormond Street
London
WC1N 3HZ

Volume copyright
© B.T. Batsford Ltd, 2021
Essay text © Elain Harwood, 2021
Text copyright © Stefi Orazi, 2021
Photography © Julian Ward (pp. 28–82);
© Mary Gaudin (pp. 88–149)

Design: Stefi Orazi Studio
Commissioning Editor: Lucy Smith
Assistant Editor: Lilly Phelan

ISBN: 9781849945943

A CIP catalogue record for this book is available
from the British Library.

10 9 8 7 6 5 4 3 2 1

Reproduction by Rival Colour Ltd, UK
Printed and bound by Leo Paper Products Ltd, China

www.pavilionbooks.com

A note on the floor plans
Plans are drawn at 1:1250. The drawings are based on
the plans published in the 1957 Golden Lane Estate
descriptive brochure produced by the Corporation of
London. In some instances exact details, such as kitchen
layout, were missing or inaccurate in the original plans.
I have tried to source accurate information but this has
not always been possible and plans should be used as
a guide only.

Image credits
p.1, p.18 (bottom), p.20 From the collection of Polly Powell
p.7 (top), p.22 (bottom) John Maltby/RIBA Collections
p.8 Peter King/Stringer/Getty
p.10 (top) © Museum of London; (bottom) British Library
p.13, p.23 © London Metropolitan Archives,
City of London
p.15 (top) RIBA Collections
p.17 (bottom), p. 22 (top), p.24 Architectural Press
Archive/RIBA Collections
p.18 (top) Popperfoto/Getty
pp.151–158 © Stefi Orazi Studio

Acknowledgements
The author would like to extend her special thanks to
the residents of Golden Lane Estate who generously let
us photograph their homes, and to those that kindly gave
up their time to allow me to interview and photograph
them—especially amid the Covid-19 pandemic. A special
thanks is due to photographers Mary Gaudin for her
excellent and sympathetic architectural photography,
and to Julian Ward for his generosity, flexibility and
sensitive portraiture photography. The author would
also like to express her sincere thanks to Elain Harwood
for her introductory essay, and to the publishing team
at Batsford.

Cover image
View of the estate from Golden Lane, 1958.
© Popperfoto/Getty

Frontispiece
From Christoph Bon's personal collection.